FREEDOM TO HO

Edited by Alan Falconer, Enda McDonagh
& Seán Mac Reamoinn

Freedom To Hope?

A FESTSCHRIFT
FOR AUSTIN FLANNERY, O.P.

GABRIEL DALY
MAURA HYLAND
NIVARD KINSELLA
MARGARET MacCURTAIN
LOUIS McREDMOND
CÉLINE MANGAN
KEVIN O'KELLY

the columba press

the columba press
84 Lakelands Avenue, Blackrock, Co. Dublin

First edition 1985
Typography and cover design
by Liam Miller
Cover artwork by Eddie McManus
Page make-up by Robert Healy
Printed in Ireland by
Mount Salus Press

ISBN 0 948183 10 1

Contents

Introduction

The essays in this volume have been written and assembled to a dual purpose. They are offered as a *festschrift* to Father Austin Flannery on the occasion of his sixtieth birthday, and to celebrate the pioneering work in which he has been engaged for nearly thirty years as editor of *Doctrine and Life*, and, more generally, of Dominican Publications.

It is no exaggeration to say that along with its still flourishing contemporary *The Furrow*, founded and long edited by the late great J. G. McGarry of Maynooth, *Doctrine and Life* has been a main agent of renewal in the Irish Church. And in so far as Ireland was not totally unprepared for the *bouleversement* of Vatican II, or totally unaware of the significance of its proceedings, this was almost entirely due to these two journals and their editors.

Flannery had also, from the early sixties, been at work on another, more informal level. Aided and abetted by his friend, the late Jack Dowling (philosopher, broadcaster, socialist), he brought together a company of somewhat unruly Christians for the raising and arguing of awkward questions, who soon learned not to expect easy answers. This is not the place to tell the story of this fraternity (*cum* sorority) which bore no title — but several unflattering nicknames: it continued to flourish until well after the council.

The idea of a *festschrift* came from among the group's survivors, but it was quickly realised that its recipient would not be best pleased with a mere pious garland of praise, however graciously he might accept it. And so we thought to honour him in attempting to serve a second aim: to present a portrait, admittedly partial, of where and how we stand now, twenty years after the council's end, and on the eve of the synod called by Pope John Paul II to reconsider its effects.

And so our essayists report on some seven areas in the life of the Church in the order in which the conciliar documents dealing with them were promulgated, and as published in *Vatican Council II: Conciliar and Post-Conciliar Documents*[1]. As the exercise is essentially one of self-examination, all our essayists, save one, are of the Roman Catholic obedience.

1

They include, then, two religious sisters, a laywoman, three laymen, a Presbyterian minister, a monk, a friar, and a diocesan priest. It may be noted that, with one exception, the essays are written by people who were adults before the council, and in whose lives it has been a landmark. But we append an epilogue by a young woman of the conciliar generation who, accordingly, represents the majority of Irish Catholics today!

In offering our partial portrait as a contribution to that 'reconsideration' of the council which the pope called for, we are aware that in doing so we may be dubbed 'unrepresentative', and lacking in such standing or authority as would entitle us to speak for the Irish Church.

Certainly, if authority be seen as solely within the hierarchical order, we are, as editors and essayists, innocent of it; certainly, our standing as a group is no more and no less than that of the individuals who form it; most certainly, we claim no representative status, even if some among us hold, or have held, canonical office.

But to dwell on this would be to miss the point of our modest enterprise. We offer no challenge to Church leadership. Our challenge, if challenge is the word for it, is addressed to the Church as a whole — baptised, married, ordained; old and young; devout and alienated — to God's People in Ireland.

But we would prefer to call it an invitation: to see ourselves as depicted in the portrait, to learn from the events portrayed and the successes or failures recorded, and to act as the situation would seem to demand. Again the word 'portrait' is hardly adequate — we would need to draw on the metaphor of film or video to reflect the *kinesis* of change in growth. Our most immediate aim must be a degree of self-awareness so that we who *are* the Church can measure our response to that 'universal call to holiness' which, as the great constitution *Lumen Gentium* so clearly states, is the common vocation of the People of God.

Not that any amount of self-awareness can fathom the Mystery of the Church. However, we do well to remember that 'we can never understand *everything* about a mystery but we can understand something'.

And this Mystery of the Church is, to use the words of the constitution 'in the nature of sacrament — a sign and an instrument, that is, of communion with God and of unity with all men ... for by communicating his Spirit, Christ mystically constitutes as his body those brothers of his who are called together from every nation'.

2

The Church, then, is at once the sacrament of Christ and the sacrament of the world. It is the great Sign of the Kingdom *in* this world, and the form of the Sign is human community and human institution. And these two, frail and fallible as they are, are ever in need of self-discovery, of conversion ... *semper reformanda*.

Both as community and as institution the Church was and continues to be profoundly affected by the proceedings of Vatican II. Indeed, not alone in *Lumen Gentium* but also in several other documents, community has been seen to have received its Magna Carta, while the institution, if not downgraded, lost much of its former formidable sovereignty. Such a view, while understandable on a superficial level, lacks the insight of experience. What is true is that — as in the old Scripture/Tradition dilemma — community and institution are seen to be complementary and inseparable. Community cannot exist without some institutional integument, no more than soul without body: and an institution that does not serve community is a Frankenstein's monster.

All our essayists have written from a lived experience of community: religious and secular, denominational and ecumenical, liturgical and political. And it is from within this experience that they offer their comments and criticisms of those structures and practices which are meant to serve community. But communities as well as institutions are made of human material, and in the long run we are left with the weak children of Eve and Adam, who can achieve great good — and great ill.

In the last analysis, the community and institutions of the Second Vatican Council were a channel for the Holy Spirit to move through his Church and his world. In him who is all Truth and all Love we try to tell the truth in love. To him we look for the freedom to hope.

Alan D. Falconer
Enda McDonagh
Seán Mac Reamoinn

4th October 1985

SEÁN MAC REAMOINN

Renewal or Revision?

1. SUCCESS STORY?

On the face of it, liturgical renewal has been *the* success story of
Vatican II in Ireland. The new norms have been generally well
implemented and accepted. The vernacular is taken for granted,
both in Irish and English, there is little nostalgia for the 'old
ways', and no Latin Mass society.

Mass attendance figures are still over-all very high and, while
the quality of participation varies widely, at its weakest it com-
pares more than favorably with pre-council days: at its best it is
very impressive indeed. The days of the silent congregation are
numbered, if not over, and the people's voice is heard, even —
mirabile dictu — in song! Lay readers are common, and include
both men and women, as do 'special ministers' at the Eucharist.
Communicants of all ages and backgrounds seem as happy with
them as they are with Communion in the hand (generally available to all who choose it).

They have also responded to the greater availability of the
Sacrament: Mass without Communion for the people is now a
forgotten practice. Lunch-time, and especially evening, Celebrations have been facilitated by the virtual disappearance of the
Eucharistic fast. Also, the multiplicity of Masses, often at the
same time at different altars, once common at least in urban and
conventual churches, has yielded to the restored rite of conceleb-
ration.

The communal dimension has become a noteworthy and welcome feature in the celebration of the other sacraments. Baptism
has ceased to be a 'private' affair, and the absence of the mother
(once regarded as normal) would now be unthinkable, except in
very special circumstances: similarly, parents are now made
welcome at Confirmation! Communal celebrations of Penance
are still rare, but occasional 'penitential services', involving rite
two, have proved popular.

The ministerial role of bride and groom in marriage, always
taught in theory, has now become clear: the function of the
principal witnesses has also been clarified (as has that of god-

5

parents and sponsors in the rites of initiation). The ordaining of bishops, priests, and deacons, has become more meaningful if less 'mysterious'.

But one is tempted to single out the Sacrament of the Sick as the one where renewal has most clearly taken place and been accepted. No longer popularly regarded as a kind of holy death certificate, it is happily received by many whose immediate hope is for restoration to health. The traditional link with the Eucharist has been made to include family and friends, and the whole celebration is, at its best, indicative of a renewed ministry to the sick and disabled.

The Sacrament of the Sick is not the only one where the centrality of the Eucharist is commonly made explicit. Marriages are now usually celebrated during Mass, as is Confirmation, and, sometimes, adult Baptism: it has of course always been the case with ordinations. It might indeed be suggested that the link between Penance and the Eucharist has been weakened rather than strengthened, but this is arguably more apparent than real, relating to a discipline often misunderstood, rather than to any theological praxis.

Undoubtedly, one of the most striking effects of the renewal has been a new and heightened awareness of the importance of God's Word as the essential liturgical complement of sacramental action. The Mass-going Irish know their Bible today as never before, even if in this at least, they still lag far behind their Protestant fellow-countrymen. This is of course principally due to the use of the two vernaculars, and it may not be out of place here to pay tribute to the devotion and scholarship which have, if belatedly, produced the new Gaelic Bible.

Along with all this has come a greatly increased homiletic output, contrasting quite strongly with pre-conciliar practice. While preaching at Mass was, of course, very common indeed, it was possible to 'avoid' a sermon in many churches by attending an early Mass: ironically, Communion was usually given to the people at the earlier Celebrations only, so that the sacramentally devout were often deprived of the Word. And it can be more generally stated that the sermon was, as often as not, lacking in homiletic content, and with but little bearing on the day's liturgy. Nowadays, a Sunday Mass without a homily is a rarity, and, even on weekdays, many celebrants feel bound to comment, however briefly, on the readings.

And so at last I have come to mention the one whose ministry is still central to our worship, however much he and we depend

6

on auxiliary ministries. In fact, his task has become incomparably more difficult, more demanding, more delicate, than it was twenty five years ago.

My present reference is only to the liturgical task. This was formerly seen as solely a matter of priestly 'power' conferred by ordination, of grace hardly in need of nature. The theory and practice of *opus operatum* left little room for gifts, talents, skills of a personal or subjective kind.

Nowhere was this more evident than in the celebration of what we have come to know as the Liturgy of the Word. Texts were read (sometimes sung) in Latin with little attempt at *communication*: quite often, of course, this was achieved by a repetition of some of the Scripture readings in the verncular. But this was regarded as extra-liturgical, though of catechetical value. My point here is that the 'decent obscurity' of the Latin made no demands on the minister as to clarity, intelligibility, even audibility — let alone interpretation or presentation. This, with the coming of the vernacular, is now changed, changed utterly.

I nearly added: a terrible duty was born! So it may well have seemed to many among the first generation of pastors, adapting to the new ways. That they did so adapt, whether enthusiastically or in reluctant obedience, deserves our admiration. For little in their training and discipline had prepared them for this: hitherto, Mass and the sacraments had called for devotion, and for fidelity to the rubric — little more. A good singing voice could, on occasion, be an asset, but the exercise of other gifts (or indeed of personality) belong *outside* the sanctuary in the wider pastoral arena. Preaching could be an apparent exception, but this was more often a matter of moral guidance — rarely of liturgical or theological reflection.

But slowly, steadily, and at times, no doubt, painfully, the change was made. The agent of the *opus operatum* has gradually assumed his role as president of the liturgical assembly, facing his alloted constituency of God's people, and engaging all his resources, of nature as well as of grace, in bringing them God's gifts of word and sacrament.

The total achievement, involving pastors and people, is far from perfect — as we shall see — and may indeed be flawed in some quite radical ways. It remains, nevertheless, remarkably impressive — all the more so when we recall the general state of liturgical awareness in Ireland in the decades immediately preceding the council. The ferment of ideas, already burgeoning in the 1930s, which matured after the second world war, had a wide influence on pastoral as well as intellectual life in France, Germany and the Low Countries, and to a lesser extent in Great Britain and the United States. But it left the Irish Church untouched — or very nearly. One or two prophetic voices there were, and thanks to Austin Flannery, O.P., and the late J. G. McGarry, readers of *Doctrine and Life* and *The Furrow* became not unaware of what was happening, were to some extent prepared for change, and even began to speculate on how such change might affect the noble monolith of Catholic life in Ireland.

The first fruits of the movement for renewal came with the restoration of the Easter Vigil, first offered experimentally in 1949, and later becoming the corner stone of a renewed Paschal celebration covering the whole *Triduum sacrum*, and made mandatory in 1955. This delighted some of us, bewildered others, and was considered with grave misgivings by the Irish bishops, who are on record as having made a strong plea to the Holy See for an indult which would allow the old rite to continue here. Providentially, they were refused.

In retrospect, it is difficult to see why the bishops panicked. The 'new' rite would today seem quite conservative, and it was still subject to the discipline of the Latin language. But, in fact, it held the seeds of much of what has since come to flower, and in this sense was truly revolutionary — as well as giving most Irish people their first experience of evening Mass, with Communion for all (on Holy Thursday).

In the event, prophets of gloom and 'practical' critics of the new Paschal liturgy were discomfited: it was received by the great mass of the faithful with real goodwill and not a little enthusiasm. And to all with eyes to see and ears to hear it presaged the death of that old excuse for *immobilismè*: 'The people don't want it ... '

The lesson did not appear to have been learned by the bishops — or most of them — in their first approach to the council. Nor, in fairness, did they expect any radical change in liturgy, or elsewhere in the Church's life. And when the constitution *Sacrosanctum concilium* was, after long debate, finally promulgated at the end of the second session, in December 1963, even the most sanguine among our few native reformers were sceptical, not to say pessimistic, in their view of the likely pace and substance of the Irish Church's response.

They were wrong. But understandably so. It may suffice to mention that the then Archbishop of Dublin, whose diocese was by far the largest in Ireland, and was generally seen as the dominant figure in the Irish Church, was known to be 'cool' on renewal, and though he would loyally accept the letter of the new law, he was not likely to be an enthusiastic force for change.

What nobody foresaw was that, as things turned out, energetic leadership *did* come from another archbishop: the new Primate of All Ireland, William Conway. He was, perhaps, an unlikely reformer, but his fundamental conservativism was tempered by a sharp sense of reality: to put it crudely, he saw how the liturgical wind was blowing, that it was no passing blast, and that the Church in Ireland must bend to it. And he persuaded his fellow-bishops, with one or two notable exceptions, to his view.

It should be said too of Conway that he was fascinated by ideas on the march. He was also a man of real, if old-fashioned, piety and his devotion to the Church universal was genuine. I am convinced that he saw the exercise of power as a service to the Church. He certainly exerted himself mightily in laying the foundations of liturgical renewal. Some of us at the time regarded him as over-cautious, but he was always concerned not to go too fast or too far ahead of his allies and supporters, not to mention the general body of the faithful. And in fact, in implementing Roman decisions and instructions — conciliar, synodal or administrative — there was little or no dragging of feet. In setting the pace for change, the primate's judgement was faultless.

Among those bishops who were Conway's closest allies was Cahal B. Daly, who succeeded to the see of Ardagh and Clonmacnoise in 1967, and was later translated to Down and Connor. As chairman of the art and architecture sub-committee of the liturgical commission he led a vigorous campaign to provide suitable architectural and artisitic settings for the new liturgy, involving both new buildings and the adaptation of existing sanctuaries. In this area, as in the general movement for renewal, Ireland had been notoriously out of step with contemporary trends, and, with a few striking exceptions, such churches as had been built in the quarter-century before the council were determinedly conservative in design (while often oddly eclectic in external decoration). And while we could boast of some outstanding artists in stone, glass, and ceramics, their work was rarely given ecclesiastical patronage. But slowly, very slowly, pastoral taste did begin to improve (or, at least, to change), again largely due to the influence of McGarry and Flannery.

I suppose there is hardly a sanctuary in the country now which has not undergone adaptation, and all new churches are built to

9

conform with the new norms. Nowhere is the change more striking than in Dublin, once the bastion of conservatism: after a slow start the old has been made new, and the new are unmistakeably post-conciliar. This was mainly brought about by the late Archbishop Dermot Ryan, in whose twelve years of office (1972-84) some sixty churches were built to serve a rapidly growing metropolitan population. And in each of these, crowded Sunday congregations come to Mass celebrated in a language and a manner to which even the older worshippers have long been accustomed and with which their children have grown up. Indeed, since the population explosion of the 'sixties and 'seventies means that half of our people are under twenty-five, only a minority of our Catholic church-goers remember the Latin Mass.

2. YES, BUT ...

The Constitution on the Liturgy was the first fruit of Vatican II, and its promulgation was greeted with delight by all who looked forward to a new age of renewal. I remember how, on that December evening in 1963, I set about about collecting comments on the occasion for Irish radio listeners from council fathers, *periti*, and others. Among those I approached was Hans Küng: he received me courteously and agreed to record, but as he spoke I was dismayed to find that he did not, apparently, share the general enthusiasm of his fellow 'progressives'. Did he then find the document unsatisfactory? By no means, on the whole he thought it was excellent. But ...? But — it came too late, perhaps a hundred years too late, at least for Europe. His point was that a renewed liturgy could and should be a dynamic force for the renewal of the worshipping community, but alas! such a community no longer existed, or only marginally, in the traditionally Catholic countries.

With, he said, one exception. In Ireland, an authentic sacramental life was general among the Catholic population, and here, indeed, renewal could be immensely fruitful not only at home, but, because of our missionary tradition, wherever the Irish Church was planted. So it was up to us!

But, were *we* up to *it*? Well, from what I have already written here, it might appear that we were and are. The churches are as full as ever — or nearly as full, and the congregations seem to have made the transition smoothly to the new ways.

So, then, has Küng's vision been realised: is Ireland the model of liturgical renewal, a community whose life in worship shines like a candle to the world? Have we become exemplars of that

10

'noble simplicity' which the council enjoined, of 'sweet and living love for sacred scripture', of 'unity in holiness', of 'holding fast in our lives what we have grasped by our faith'?

Clearly, if regrettably, the answer must be: no! Probably, it could never be otherwise. But ideals, even if beyond our grasp, are worth looking towards, and it can be useful to measure ourselves against them.

In the matter of liturgical revision, we have undoubtedly come a long way, but revision, even reform, does not always mean renewal. The letter, the rubric, may change, while the spirit remains bound. A clear examination of conscience of called for, to discover if, in the classic words of another liturgy, 'we have left undone those things which we ought to have done', and perhaps 'done those those things which we ought not to have done'.

Happily, it would be untrue to add, 'and there is no health in us'. For all our faults and failings there is not a little to be grateful for in the life of the Irish Church: a new awareness of and commitment to human needs; an emphasis on love and hope rather than sin and fear; some sense of Church, mission, ministry; some care for the beauty of holiness.

The list is by no means exhaustive, nor could one suggest that such good things were not to be found in pre-conciliar days. But they have become at once more central and more widely diffused. And this may surely be claimed as fruit of a renewal which was no mere revision.

But our immediate concern is the negative side, the sins of commission, and especially, omission. On both counts we have plenty to be ashamed of, but, again, rather than attempt an inclusive blacklist, I would think it more useful to consider some of the more obvious symptoms of ill-health, in the hope of diagnosing the roots of the trouble.

First of all, some of the commonest accusations against the new liturgy. It has (we are told) lost the dimension of *mystery*; language is flat, dull, lacking in poetry (this more often about English than Irish); the new music is mostly junk; beautiful sanctuaries and whole churches have been ruined; there's a false *bonhomie*, as in the kiss of peace, but also too often in sermons; too much noise and fuss.

On a different level from such blanket criticism, there is a fair amount of dissatisfaction, even, and perhaps especially, among enthusiasts and 'insiders', mostly in relation to *performance*. This might perhaps be best expressed as detecting the emergence of a new ritualism, a revival of *opus operatum* attitudes, by which

11

we have exchanged old rubrics for new, and which reduce praying, reading, participating, to a mechanical level. Preparation, such as the study of texts, is seen to be neglected, as celebrants rely on the skills of experience to provide a reading which, technically flawless, fails to communicate.

From another point of view, but again not one of general opposition to the reforms, one hears complaints about a lack of reverence and dignity, a neglect of the value of silence, leading to an atmosphere not conducive to prayer. As in the previous criticism, the fault is generally seen as being that of the celebrant.

He also comes in for a good deal of criticism as a homilist, the range being predictably wide. He is either too academic or too trivial, too remote or too intimate, 'above people's heads' or too down-to-earth, pompous or slangy in diction, playing safe with generalities or playing politics. He rarely pleases, or, if he does, nobody tells him.

Here I might insert a needle of my own. There are certain primary social occasions — Baptisms, weddings, funerals — which can offer a particular opportunity to the celebrant as *persona ecclesiae*. Both in his homily and in his whole liturgical performance he can bring joy or comfort to those most closely involved — in a word, he can be a timely and effective bearer of the Good News. And he may reach hearts and minds who never heard it before, or never really listened .... Or, he can be a ritual robot, leaving both the happy and the sorrowful untouched by word or action, and confirming the alienated in their persuasion that it's all a load of old rubbish, with no bearing on real life. Boredom — or worse — rules.

Mention of boredom reminds me that this is one of the reasons most often quoted for what is one of the saddest symptoms suggesting that something is very wrong. I mean the steady drift away from worship of so many young people. I do not intend here to rehearse or assess statistics, nor would I presume to attempt any general over-view of such relevant factors as the heightened pace of cultural change, adolescent nonconformism, the competing attractions of the 'cults' and of certain neo fundamentalist groups, as well as simple, plain apathy. But if we believe in the centrality of liturgy in the life of the Christian community, the drift must be seen as a serious sign: especially if, as appears to be so often the case, it carries with it some of the most sensitive, intelligent and caring of our young people — not just the lazy and the *lumpen*.

The other sad symptom, and not only sad but deeply shameful,

12

is, of course, the frightening discrepancy between out church-going and so much of our social behaviour. That there will always be a gap between prayer and practice is inevitable, part of the human condition, and, in Christian history, it has often widened to the breadth of an abyss where many have perished: a scandal and a betrayal of the Gospel.

Are we really that bad in Ireland today? And, specifically, are 'good' Catholics just so many hypocrites? No: it's not that simple. The blameless, even heroic, lives of the faithful could be counted, perhaps, in their thousands. But a range of crimes against God and neighbour darken the picture: from greed and exploitation, to cruel neglect of the weak and helpless, to the corruption of the innocent and intimidation of the defenceless, to violent crime — not excluding murder itself, often wearing the dress of a sick and perverted patriotism.

If the 'just society' is still our aim, it remains a long way off, and our slow movement towards it is not hastened by political cowardice and social self-indulgence. And we who share the responsibility for this state of affairs, or most of us, are seen to be members of the worshipping community who are called to be a light to the world.

And the council tells us that 'it is through the liturgy, especially, that the faithful are enabled to express in their lives, and manifest to others the mystery of Christ, and the real nature of the true Church ....

'The liturgy daily builds up those who are in the Church, making of them a holy temple of the Lord, a dwelling-place for God in the Spirit to the mature measure of the fullness of Christ. At the same time it marvellously increases their power to preach Christ and thus show forth the Church, a sign lifted up among the nations....'

Do the splendid words ring sadly hollow? If, as we must admit, they do, where does the weakness lie? Or, as John Betjeman might put it: How did the devil get in?

Not that there is any immediate need for a recourse to the demonic explanation. Human failings and errors account for a lot. If we consider some of the more peripheral faults found with our liturgical *praxis*, we can at best plead youth and inexperience — in the *art* of worship we are all apprentices, and all of us under twenty-five. Yes, most of the liturgical translations (apart from Scripture) lack vitality and we still have a lot to learn about public praying and reading. Yes, a lot of the new music *is* junk, not because it's new or in a folk idiom: too much of it is bad *of its kind*. Yes, the re-shaping of sanctuaries has sometimes lacked sensitivity and even decent taste — and some new churches are just architectural clichés.

That reform should beget philistinism is, of course, nothing new. And the misshapen progeny has unhappily too often survived its parent, not least in the history of religious reform. The iconoclasts are always with us.

It is also regrettably true that the principles of reform are often, perhaps usually, seen as effecting a closure of options. It becomes a rigid question of 'either/or'. Thus when Latin ceased to be mandatory in Catholic worship, it was commonly and promptly expelled from sanctuary and choir. Fortunately, even in Ireland, there are occasional oases of sanity where the glories of plain chant and classical polyphony are still allowed to enhance the liturgy. And at such times as Holy Week or Christmas midnight Mass, a Latin *Gloria* or *Adeste*, tentatively introduced in a vernacular celebration, evokes an unexpectedly happy response ... not to mention the tuneful roar that can still proclaim the *Credo*.

It is perhaps too much to expect that a long tradition of going by the rubric should dissolve in one generation, or that all the skills and charisms, all the sureness of touch, which the presidential role demands could be acquired overnight. Much has been done to give liturgical studies a central place 'among the compulsory and major courses in seminaries and religious houses of studies' as the conciliar constitution prescribes, and in welcome contrast to the almost marginal position only a few years ago when it was regarded merely as a kind of sacred grammar. The good effect of this is apparent among many of the more recently ordained: clearly the orientation and emphasis of their formation has been soundly pastoral. But mastery of the new 'art of celebrating' (McGarry's phrase) comes slowly, sometimes painfully — sometimes never. In homiletics too, art is less easily learned than science. So the breaking of the Word may not always touch the heart of the bride, or the bereaved, or the half-believer in his uncertain solidarity.

Here indeed we do well to remember the promised gift — not perhaps of eloquence, but of a share in the inspiration of the Good News: 'for it is not you who speak but the Spirit of the Father speaking through you'. And this is the reality on which all ministry, of Word as of sacrament, is grounded.

But there is a call as well as a promise in the reality, the call to that 'royal priesthood' which is our common baptismal inheritance, and in which we come to share in Christ, the Sacrament of God: a call also to the ministry of those ordained to the high service of the sacramental community. And call demands response, of heart and mind and will. This response, in worship and service, is at once the deepest realisation of our humanity and the highest activity to which we can aspire, *leitourgia*: the work of the People of God.

3 OBLIGATION OR CELEBRATION

The people's work is the people's duty: this cannot be gainsaid. It is also the people's privilege, their joy, their glory, their fulfilment — or should be. It heals their wounds, lightens their darkness, restores them to wholeness, and makes them one with each other in the Spirit.

But it might appear that none of this is of great concern. Worship, liturgy, is above all a *duty*, and a good Christian is to be judged on how he fulfils that duty, according to the rules and laws laid down. I do not think that this is an exaggeration or distortion of the 'traditional' attitude, dominant until very recently, and still current among many, perhaps most, Catholics. And not among Catholics only: the dedication of Sunday to compulsory worship is or was one of the hall-marks of Protestant cultures, although without the sanction of 'mortal sin', invoked as the penalty of truants and strays from the Roman obedience.

Our vocabulary was riddled with the idea that adoration, prayer, even participation in the Eucharist, were matters of obligation, of obedience, with a penal dimension. Thinking of phrases like 'fulfilling your obligation', 'doing your Easter duty', 'you don't *have* to go to Mass today', one wonders at the strength of a devotion which survived such cold sterilities, not to mention the undervaluing of God's Word which enjoined Mass attendance as 'of obligation' only from the offertory to the priest's Communion! And it should be realised that the rules were taken with appalling seriousness, to the extent that to 'miss' Mass, or to be 'late' was, objectively at least, a mortal sin, in the same category as murder ... To say the very least of it, such a discipline was bound to produce a very unbalanced idea of what worship might mean, of sacrament and sacrifice, and of God himself.

One has to ask whether, in fact, such an understanding or misunderstanding of the creature's duty to his Creator, as of the redeemed to the Redeemer, is even compatible with that celebration of both creation and redemption 'to which the Christian people ... have a right and *obligation* by reason of their Baptism'.

15

I have italicised the word 'obligation' in this quotation from the Liturgy Constitution, because it at once casts a new light on the word, and, thus, answers our question. For of course the idea of duty, *at its deepest* and always correlated to *right*, is not alone in harmony with the idea of celebration but gives it substance. Thus, the celebration of human love in sexuality involves the fulfilment of a mutual duty which is also a mutual right. But this is far from the legalistic, even penal context in which words like 'duty' are too often used.

Such usage or misusage is in fact all too familiar in legal-ecclesiastical pronouncements on marriage: 'payment of the marriage debt', and other heart-warming phrases which are as far from expressing the unique meeting of man and woman, as talk of a 'holiday of obligation' is from the marriage feast of the Lamb. And we must quite simply get rid of these noxious weeds which have too long been allowed to poison our discourse, our understanding and perhaps our lives.

It is not of course simply a question of language, though language is important. We must purge our consciousness not of the sense of duty, but of that trivialising distortion which turns God's free gift into a kind of spiritual bank-loan. We must liberate ourselves, not from law but from legalism which is the yoke of law: only then will we be truly free to celebrate.

KEVIN O'KELLY

Communication in the Church

In Ireland as elsewhere communication is not just about talking and listening. Lovers and mystics can have the most profound communication without saying a word. The teaching of the Second Vatican Council has, among other things, emphasised that, in order to communicate, each must be present to the other. It means we must take each other seriously with all our various preoccupations, including the preparation of the Kingdom. The mass media of communication can indeed assist in these endeavours, but their usefulness can be exaggerated.

In Ireland, perhaps especially in Ireland, most Christians derive convictions about the Kingdom and about the Kingdom to come not from the media but from racial memory and the example of their peers. Most of us have inherited a faith and are content to live by it. Media reports of theological debate at the Second Vatican Council had little impact on the daily lives of adult Irish Catholics who had grown up contentedly, guided by the certainties of an authoritarian Church. In any case the council debates were of little obvious relevance to daily Christian living. For many, indifference to the goings-on at the council was reinforced by the late Archbishop John Charles McQuaid of Dublin when he reassured his people that nothing that had happened during the four council years need disturb the tranquility of the their Christian lives. This was welcome reassurance for a community that was only just becoming aware of the intellectual unrest abroad in the decade of the 'sixties.

The change in life-style implicit in the teachings of the council was a question of making all things new, not just talking about them. And the Christian community in Ireland often prefers talk to action. Of course, some change did come, but congregations needed a great deal of persuasion that it was needed; and in the end they were convinced that alteration in Church discipline would be good or tolerable only when they had person-to-person assurance from a parish priest they knew and trusted. Above all, the priest had the Power. My grandmother used to watch a Protestant clergyman going up to visit a sick friend of hers, and

17

she was sorrowful: 'Sure, what can he do?' She sighed and explained to her young grandson that the clergyman had not got the Power. That power is real in many ways and sometimes resented when it spills over into worldly affairs.

If ceremonial changes were accepted in the liturgy, similar acceptance was not extended to other implications of the theology from which these changes derived. Irish Catholics, like most Christians, especially those of the pre-council tradition, were not concerned with theology. They did not need it to communicate with the invisible God, understanding that, faithfully observed, ritual guides the soul to heaven. The priest is in charge of the ritual: the Minister of the Mysteries. Over the decades, newspapers, radio, and television could report new ideas and indeed these might sometimes be relevant or interesting. But they could not convey grace. They had not the Power. They were, therefore, irrelevant to the business of 'making one's soul'; of getting to heaven.

Especially for those who grew up before the council, a deep faith derived from history and long tradition is a spiritual strength and in some ways a worldly weakness. Seldom more than a generation removed from rural origins, it is a faith that tends to make but a hazy distinction between the temporal and spiritual, between God's earth and God's heaven. It views death hopefully as a rite of passage, and heaven as the destination of each man and woman. The Church keeps the passage safe, the sacraments the gate of heaven ajar. So, whatever unorthodox views there are about religious affairs, it is thought well to communicate them discreetly.

Meanwhile the illusion of dialogue had been preserved in the media. Many a criticism about religious and religion has been made on radio, television, and in print by journalists, minor politicians and other well-recognised people of no authority. But there has been little of such talk from people in power or in pursuit of power. Communication of this nature has been minimal because whatever private thoughts there may have been (except for a few notable exceptions among priests, people and politicians), it has been considered imprudent publicly to offend religious sensibilities.

Interested intellectuals had their *Furrow*s and their *Doctrine and Life*s and *Concilium* and all the rest, but the ideas discussed in these publications had for many years little impact on the public. When they did impinge, perhaps a decade after Paul VI closed the last council session in St Peter's, it was mainly on the minds of young men and young women now emerging dazed and disillusioned from the swinging 'sixties into the depressed 'seventies. The impact came by a roundabout route: by way of Latin America and Africa. The people there, good Christians as most of them were, were already just as convinced as the Irish that they were destined for God. But their poverty and oppression was so extreme that those who went on mission to them, even from tranquil Catholic congregations, accepted that in those far countries social change was imperative if injustice was to be overcome, and that this involved a radical new appraisal of the Gospel message. They found that the documents of the council, in the light of the Gospel, were a rich source of ideas and intuitions which could help to liberate the people of Latin America from sin and from oppression.

But this was happening to Irish people abroad while back home the big religious experience for the adult Catholic was the use of English in the Mass, the fact that the altars were being turned round and that the priest was facing the people. Vocations declined because young men and women wanted more fundamental changes to meet the challenges of Ireland's poverty and violence. Bishops and priests issued exhortations to keep the faith, to be loyal to the pope. The pope himself came and assured the young people of Ireland that he loved them, and they rejoiced for the day. But now he is gone. The exhortations of pope, bishop and priest were published in the newspapers; they were preached from the pulpit (or, now, from the ambo), but fewer young people came to listen, and often the public address system was of poor quality.

The Church at large — the whole Christian community — mistook all this for communication. And this included those whom the council described as the People of God, who had not begun to understand — because they had never been told — that they had ideas to contribute; that the Spirit was in them too; that they were part of the grand design by which the Gospel was to be communicated. This was not emphasised in official teaching after the council. It is still not a prominent part of that teaching. So strong has been the inherited respect for priestly power and authority that it is only now, decades after the council debates, that actual perusal of the council documents has, even without benefit of further education in the slums of Sao Paolo or Santiago, convinced growing numbers of men and women of their own priesthood and of their duty to contribute to the dialogue that seeks understanding. Such a contribution involves the form-

19

ation of community without which there can be no truly inter-personal communication, and which ideally demands sacrifice of self, and begins in table fellowship: in the gathering for the breaking of bread and the prayers. During the past decade it is notably those people who were on mission abroad who have encouraged this new understanding and helped to communicate it here. Again: effective communication has to be person-to-person. The media have provided a global context for the communication. They have not brought it about.

An essentially informal encounter with the Christian mysteries was entirely natural in the slums of El Salvador where often a tin shack is the church. Irish men and women coming home from Latin America have, however, found difficulties translating their experience to parishes here; but they keep at it, believing that there is need to encourage these small group encounters as channels of grace for the community at large.

Talking to large numbers of people from a distance, from pulpit or platform, cannot be a substitute for being truly present to each of them, no more than 'presence' on television (still less in print) is a real presence at all. There is a problem, then. Quite apart from preaching in large churches, the institution is trying to use the media to 'be present' to millions. But the media purvey either fantasies or information. They cannot substitute for flesh and blood. The Word was made flesh because God saw that godliness could most efficaciously be communicated in a person-to-person way, and the whole business of human communication is — must be — based on acceptance that men and women are body-spirits and that the classical encounter between human beings is that sexual encounter within marriage where the two become one flesh. And that, according to St Paul, is an image of Christ's relationship with his Church. The media are no substitute for communication, though they can be used as a sad substitute for human intercourse.

The Vatican's Pastoral Instruction on the Means of Social Communication says this: 'Through his incarnation [Christ] utterly identified himself with those who were to receive his communication, and he gave them his message not only in words but in the whole manner of his life'. And again: 'Communication is more that the expression of ideas and the indication of emotion. At its most profound level it is the giving of self in love'. (Flannery's translation). Communication within the Christian community is then going to be so much the better inasmuch as it is person to person, body to body, spirit to spirit. Confrontation could be another word if it did not have unfortunate overtones of authoritarianism. People should face people. No. Let's be more exact: person must face person. There is no short cut. One person cannot face one million people except in the most tangential way. So, each must be on mission to the other. It is the personal witness, the personal recommendation that will be acted on rather than the impersonal. 'Come. And see.'

Of course Christian dialogue is enriched by the information conveyed through the media, or it can be. But this is not an altogether popular idea. The Vatican certainly does not favour communication by the mass media except in a very restricted sense. It has never admitted journalists to important meetings whether of council, synod or commission. Instead, it has preferred to issue handouts or give briefings with its own versions of debates within the Church. These have often been misleading, and have sometimes omitted significant contributions which spoke against the prevailing Vatican line. Vatican press officials are never perturbed when this is pointed out. Their news conferences are models of bland equanimity, and the *Osservatore Romano* (which is almost exclusively devoted to printing transcripts of the pope's speeches; it is not a newspaper) reports only the official statements at these occasions, never the questions or the answers. If any officially unauthorised fact is revealed or difficulty disclosed the *Osservatore* leaves it to be reported by The Means of Social Communication Without the Walls, where it can always be denied as being a misquotation.

Officially, though pious words are regularly said, the Vatican Press Office is never seen to act as though the Church had any need of change, and this is probably the reason why it hardly ever has anything of significance to report. It is a means of preventing news rather than announcing it. It is quite irrelevant to the Christian endeavour.

In Ireland's news media there is a cohort of interested and committed journalists (not by any means confined to people labelled 'religious affairs correspondents') who are able and willing to report Church affairs. Unfortunately, the institutional Church has not been an arena in which they could function to the best advantage — of Church or media.

There is little significant communication within the Church structures — two-way communication which would generate ideas and actions worthy of reporting. There are formal channels of communication, but they are often rusty with disuse. The conference of priests, though officially recognised, had to work for years to achieve even the beginnings of a dialogue with the bishops' conference, and it is not clear that their encounters have produced results of significance. There are many parish councils, but no evidence that any significant number have been given decisive powers in matters of importance. The national council of the the laity has not been asked to make decisions of consequence. There has never been a national pastoral council, though there have been innumerable bishops' pastorals.

Few of these have generated much debate. Again, there has been an ambivalent response: outward respect for the pastoral words but minimal action. The words have indeed carried force where there is already a degree of consensus for or against their ideas — on questions of sexual morality like abortion and divorce. But this has not been true to anything like the the same extent when they have spoken on social questions. Their major pastoral of justice, lavished with formal praise, had no significant results at least partly because it did not express a consensus which could have been derived from public consultation. In contrast, recent pastorals of the American bishops, on armaments and the economy, have been influential because the documents were the product of prolonged public debate throughout the United States. In this debate the mass media were necessary catalysts — as they could be in similar circumstances here in Ireland. The first that members of the Irish public know about pastorals is when they read about them in the newspapers. Their ideas are not canvassed; they are not invited to participate in making judgements on Church life.

The bishops meet three times a year at Maynooth, and there is a news conference afterwards at which a formal typewritten statement is issued, frequently accompanied by the comment from the spokesman that there is nothing very newsworthy to report. Under questioning, the full agenda may be revealed. However, nothing contentious ever seems to be discussed or, if is is, there is complete unanimity among all bishops present. Episcopal dialogue does not seem to take place. At any rate, answers to difficult questions at Maynooth news conferences are usually quoted either from the Code of Canon Law or the latest directive from the Vatican. One-way communication seems to be the norm: Rome to Dublin. Officially a crisis is never admitted even though the bishops' own research suggests that many young men and women are alienated and that there is extreme confusion in the minds of younger Catholics about such basic questions as the existence of God or the divinity of Christ. The young have not now the comfort of pre-conciliar certainties.

Of course, the episcopal press office functions efficiently, and bishops make themselves freely available for interview. But formal media-events cannot substitute for regular, structured inter-communication on matters of substance between all members of the entire Christian community and especially between all the people of the Roman Catholic community and their priests. Media appearances of episcopal spokesmen merely create the illusion of dialogue though the illusion is often very polished. Spokesmen have had time, since the council, to learn how to use the mass media — usually to reassure the public that all is well.

The performance is sometimes quite brilliant: most significantly in the official Catholic Church presentation to the hearings of the New Ireland Forum and especially in their observations about the relationship between Church and State. Their formal written submission was careful to qualify acceptance of 'a justifiable political pluralism' with the observation that 'divorced from its relation to the common good it [pluralism] tends towards division and disintegration'. However, under questioning at the Forum, the Church establishment's firm conviction that it could properly define the common good was magnificently waffled away. In the same way, in television and radio interviews, the Church position on inter-Church marriage is sweetly reasonable. There is, therefore, continuing speculation why the Church of Ireland protests so constantly at what it sees as a great lack of charity in the administration of the canon law.

Again: the media are no substitute for useful communication between the Churches. The Church of Ireland has often publicly regretted its inability to communicate its point of view even to its own people, let alone to the public at large. So it could be argued that the Roman Catholic Church is too clever by half about communicating its message while the other Churches are not yet half clever enough.

However, there is now the beginnings of a climate of change as younger bishops, priests and people begin genuinely to exchange views on questions of importance. In contrast, for instance, to the uncharitable exchanges right and left during the debate on abortion, discussion about the moral implications of genetic engineering have begun here in an atmosphere of monastic calm at Glenstal Abbey, with participation by bishops from the the Anglican and Roman Catholic traditions, as well as other interested and qualified people. And again, in the recently charged atmosphere — as the Dáil was debating contraception — another of the younger bishops could oppose the idea but say also, 'We have not the fulness of truth'. Young people are, therefore, beginning to listen: to have the Gospel preached to them in a language they can accept. At a Dublin seminary recently a young woman finished a year-long course in ministry. She is an agnostic, but she chose to enhance her career as a social worker under the guidance of a priest who had been on mission among the poor abroad. At the base, genuine dialogue is beginning.

There have been regular official appeals for more vocations to the religious life, but a vocations director has been heard to say that a front page picture of a nun arrested for siding with travelling people against the Gardaí was the best advertisement for vocations he had seen in years. There are some ways in which the media have been of service in providing, as it were, vicarious inter-personal communication. The nun and the Garda were in a very real inter-personal confrontation, and perhaps this is why the vocations director found the message so clear and powerful.

Communication, therefore, is a risky business since it involves dialogue with those of even violently opposing views; and in recent years it has been a risk that neither Church, State, nor political party, in Ireland or elsewhere, has often been willing to take. This failure seriously to communicate is doubly true in that nether world of factional violence in our country where the antagonists have so morally or physically intimidated even their own followers that they can speak publicly with a cynical disregard for truth.

However, the hierarchical structure is so firmly rooted in the Roman Catholic tradition that when you write about communication in the Church you inevitably write about bishops and *their* communications. But, despite what has been said, it is possible that bishops may have weakened their own authority by spreading it too thinly. Could it be that over-emphasis on the importance of person-to-person communication on the bishop's parish visitation might diminish the respect and authority due to the parish priest himself? Should not the principle of subsidiarity apply? Is not the bishop's charism to be a symbol of manifest unity that comes from consultation with priests and people? Did not the whole world, the *oikoumene*, mourn the death of John XXIII though he stayed in the Vatican for almost the whole of his pontificate? In Ireland was not Bishop Peter Birch known and respected — and influential too — throughout the country even though he was firmly based in Kilkenny? And who can deny

Archbishop Kevin McNamara's undoubted influence on the Irish Church from his base in Dublin? But to return directly to the question of visitation: can periodic visitation substitute for ongoing, structured dialogue? Can words or actions substitute for the spirit of the man?

There are two things to say after all that. The first is that each Christian is in the business of communicating with all other Christians. The second is that the professional communicator working in the mass media is chiefly in the business of conveying facts and opinions. He or she is a go-between, and 'convey' seems a more accurate word that 'communicate'. The professional can only foster communication. He cannot substitute for inter-personal dialogue. Gradually there is a realisation by many Irish Christians (in the slums of Dublin, in the welcome given by some communities for people with mental or physical handicaps, in the care for prisoners and ex-prisoners and for the poor) that there is no substitute for the communication possible in table-fellowship that was epitomised at the Last Supper. To have true communication there must be the possibility of a response to the message communicated; even the possibility of rejection. This may be why men and women of authority in Church or State are selective about who they talk to, though, having heard his advice about going the second mile, if you went to find Christ now you might well find him drinking with British soldiers in the Shankill Road. Communication, especially communication of the Christian Gospel, involves risk. It involves walking in darkness. It involves trust. And it also involves acceptance of the possibility of betrayal.

It is unfortunately true of the synods of the universal Church that what has been fostered is merely the appearance of dialogue, often permitting the expression of new ideas but then refraining from any response to them; refusing to confront the subtlety and variety of the human condition expressed in the councils of the Church itself and revealed daily by the world-wide networks serving the same mass media which the council perceived as a divine gift to man. Increasingly, the central apparatus of Church government has been by-passing even its own established fora and hierarchical structures in its dealings with those who publicly communicate points of view it deems unorthodox. It is refusing to accept the possibility of betrayal and thereby rejecting the possibility of that love that must continually work with God in the re-creation of the universe. In the local Church here in Ireland not even the formal structures of consultation are yet in place.

However, in the small beginnings just becoming visible the Christian community is now offered yet another chance to take our own little world here by storm. But the chance is conditional on its own reformation and restructuring so that its members can work together as a people sent on pilgrimage through the world and time. To set out on a purposeful pilgrimage, people need freely to communicate with one another, to agree where they want to go and what they want to do when they get there. The Spirit is already moving among them, especially among the young and even more especially among the poor. Their voice should be listened to. It has an urgent communication for the Church and for the world.

GABRIEL DALY & ALAN FALCONER

To Be One

I: BETWEEN PRESUMPTION AND DESPAIR

Hope, it used to be said, lies mid-way between presumption and despair. Something similar might be said about the fruits of ecumenical endeavour during the twenty years after Vatican II. The achievements have been exhilarating largely because they were so unpredictable, right up to the moment when the council met. Protestants had had fifty years of ecumenical experience before Roman Catholics were permitted to join in the enterprise. Indeed the effect of the promulgation of the Decree on Ecumenism bears some resemblance to the effect produced in the fourth century Church by the conversion of the Emperor Constantine. Dialogue with 'non-Catholics' (*acatholici* was the normal word in official pronouncements) had been, like dialogue with the Roman Emperor, unthinkable. Dialogue presupposes listening as well as speaking; but listening diligently to the theological convictions and arguments of 'non-Catholics' would, before Vatican II, have constituted the sin of 'indifferentism'.

Pius XI's encyclical letter, *Mortalium Animos* (1928), gave powerful reinforcement to this attitude by effectively extinguishing the hopes which had been raised by the Malines Conversations. The pope's words were uniquely dismissive: 'It is, venerable brethren, plain why this Apostolic See will never permit its people to be present at meetings of non-Catholics: since it is not legitimate to encourage an association of Christians unless it be to foster the return of dissidents to the one true Church of Christ which in former times they unhappily deserted.'[1] To place *Mortalium Animos*, with all its bleak triumphalism, alongside Vatican II's *Unitatis Redintegratio*, on ecumenism, is to appreciate the radical character of what took place in the 1960s.

There is a generalized Catholic instinct in favour of emphasising the continuity of Church tradition. Discontinuities are often seen as an embarrassment and are consequently passed over in silence. If they cannot be passed over, they are commonly described as developments. To describe the passage from *Mor-*

27

talium Animos to Unitatis Redintegratio as 'development' is really to display a rather cavalier attitude to the normal usage of words. To put it bluntly, Catholic policy in this area was quite simply, and happily, reversed at Vatican II. The Decree on Ecumenism inaugrated a new era in Roman Catholic relations with other Christians. What was formerly unthinkable was now not merely permitted but actively encouraged. A major consequence of Vatican II's teaching on ecumenism has been that no Roman Catholic can legitimately oppose the movement for Church unity. In this respect at least the Roman Catholic magisterium gives a theoretical lead to all the Churches. The specific response of Irish Catholics matches currents apparent beyond this island.

In ecumenism, as in other theological matters, the Second Vatican Council was less a reform than a revolution; and like all revolutions it spawned revolutionaries and counter-revolutionaries. Its most notable achievement, however, was the creation of a large centre-party ready, for reasons which differed from person to person, to row in with the change of direction. What was not immediatley recognised was that the council had broken a mould, with the result that things neither could nor would ever be the same again. The integralist old guard at Vatican II saw this and despairingly sought to warn their episcopal colleagues that the proposed reforms would endanger the structure so carefully engineered in the course of the previous century by a succession of popes and their curial officers. To those who thought this way, it seemed the height of folly to tamper with a hard-achieved and carefully sacralized edifice; and according to their lights, they were perfectly correct in their diagnosis of what would inevitably happen if their warning was disregarded. The majority of the conciliar fathers, however, inspired by the élan of the period, and refusing to be intimidated by integralist warnings, produced a set of documents which sought to incorporate the views of both parties. In the interests of pacifying a powerful and vocal minority, and sometimes at the expense of inner consistency, concessions were made to the integralist standpoint; and these concessionary clauses, which often cut across the dominant thrust of the documents, are still invoked by Catholics seeking conciliar support for their stand against further reform.

As Yves Congar has noted, Vatican II 'was far more heedful of its minority which was conservative, than Vatican I had been'.[2] The point, made with characteristic restraint, is important. Integralism — the Catholic form of fundamentalism — ruthlessly denied the right to dissent from any of its governing principles. Its truths were not so much commended by argument as imposed by decree. It is this which imparts to the Lefebvre rebellion a note of self-contradiction. A radically authoritarian Catholic who is condemned by authority finds himself in a hopelessly inconsistent position. Integralism of the older sort lives on among the followers of Lefebvre, who have, let it be noted, been treated far more gently that the followers of Ignaz von Döllinger after Vatican I.

The most significant difference of approach among Roman Catholics today is to be found less between supporters and opponents of Vatican II, than between those who see the council as a still active influence and those who see it rather as a spectacular and far-reaching event in the life of the Church, but nonetheless an event which is now past history. This difference of approach may be the key to much that is happening in the Roman Catholic Church today and to many of its tensions.

Those who see the council more as an historical event than as a continuing normative influence point to the fact that twenty years is almost a generation, and that young people today quite simply think of it — when they think of it at all — as belonging to the past. For those who lived through the excitement and upheaval of the 'sixties the council will probably always remain to some extent in the realm of current affairs. In their critical moments, however, they recognize that the world has moved on and that the Church must think and act accordingly. Whatever else the continuing influence of Vatican II may be, it is emphatically not an invitation to live in the past. On the contrary, it gave us the pilgrim theme which has proved so stimulating both spiritually and pastorally: we are on the move and we look to the future. *Unitatis Redintegratio* has been superseded in many respects by regional directories, agreed statements, and the intrinsic momentum of ecumenical dialogue itself. The architects of the decree would have been agreeably astonished if, twenty years ago, they could have seen some of the agreed statements that have been appearing in the past few years.

Those who speak and act as if Vatican II were a continuing, normative and limiting influence tend to favour the argument from authority and to persist in looking for official validation of every initiative. Their appeal to its documents can be selective and tendentious (a charge which they in turn bring against their more 'liberal' opponents). Many will have been educated in the deductive procedures of scholastic thought, and will be unfamiliar with, or perhaps even opposed to, the inductive thrust of contemporary theology. One has only to compare the methodology of the Agreed Statements issued by the Anglican-Roman Catholic International Commission with the methodology of the response made to them by the Congregation for the Doctrine of the Faith in order to appreciate that we have here less a disagreement over substance than than a conflict of methodological assumptions. By way of contrast, the response of the Bishops' Conference of England and Wales to the Final Report is most heartening, not merely in the affirmative tenor of its remarks but in the bishops' appreciation that 'the substantial agreement achieved by ARCIC I has been possible because of the particular methodology adopted by the Commission.'[3] The bishops, by immediately going on to quote some words of John Paul II which commend the method adopted by the Commission, effectively block off any objection from those who regard arguments from authority as prescriptive.

Intrinsic to the methodology commended by the bishops is, of course, the actual experience of dialogue. No document can hope to supply for the absence of that experience. Many, if not most, participants in continuous dialogue recognise the existence and crucial importance of ecumenical conversion. There comes a point when one's perspectives change, and ecumenical endeavour is no longer regarded simply as a worthy but sporadic and rather minor addition to the substance of one's faith; it becomes an active element in the substantial understanding and practice of that faith. At this point 'ecclesiastical joinery' gives way to a shared search for a common truth. The production of agreed statements is indeed a necessary procedure in promoting Christian unity, but it is no substitute for active dialogue at all levels in the Church.

This observation merely reflects the perennial problem of the relationship between religious statement and the experience it seeks to describe. The deepest experiences in life are open to a variety of verbal expressions. If the linguistic formulations are allowed to become primary and to take precedence over the truths they seek to convey, there can be little hope of progress towards unity. Thus, for example, to choose the words 'memorial' and 'sacrifice' in the context of the Eucharist, and to throw them antecedently into doctrinal conflict, is to adopt a methodology which offers no ecumenical prospects or hopes. Words used in this way are instruments of division. What unites is the common search for the reality which lies behind the formula.

30

Agreed statements, then, belong to one of the more hopeful manifestations of recent inter-church relationship. The dedicated men and women who spend many hours on the construction of these statements deserve the plaudits and gratitude of us all. Though they represent their Churches, have access to the highest circles in those Churches, and receive considerable attention from the media when they issue their documents, they are nevertheless a tiny minority totally dependent for the success of their labours upon the enthusiasm and industry of others in disseminating their documents. Without such general and active co-operation, agreed statements remain merely the theological currency of like-minded people, or, in the somewhat disenchanted words of David Lapsley, a manifestation of 'the élite discussing the exotic'.[4]

If agreed statements constitute perhaps the most encouraging achievements of the past two decades, failure on the part of others, clerical and lay, to ponder, circulate, discuss, and respond to these documents constitutes perhaps the most disappointing parallel feature of these decades. It cannot be said too often that there is no substitute for real, live, and continuous dialogue not just among theologians, but among the rank and file of faithful Christians. The Churches are communicating with each other with conspicuous success, but within a specialised sector and at a rarified level. They are far less successful in communicating their achievements to the rank and file of their members; and this is largely because there is so little experiential conviction among pastors and people about the central significance of Christian unity for the evangelical thrust of Christian faith. We easily forget that is was the challenge of evangelization which led to the inauguration of the ecumenical movement in 1910.

No one can reasonably deny the Roman Catholic Church's official commitment to Church unity since Vatican II. The documentary evidence of papal and episcopal statements is abundant. What is, however, causing considerable concern in ecumenical circles is the neo-conservatism so clearly evident again in Rome. This new phenomenon would appear at first blush to be mainly a matter of internal import. A moment's reflection, however, will serve to show the impracticability of secluding internal from external factors.

Ecclesiastical tact, together with an unwillingness to become involved in the internal affairs of another Church, has restrained most ecumenically-minded Protestants and Anglicans from com-

31

menting publicly on what is happening at present in the Roman Catholic Church. Cardinal Joseph Ratzinger has not felt constrained by a similar tact. In a wide-ranging interview given to the Italian journalist, Vittorio Messori, the Prefect of the Congregation for the Doctrine of the Faith (C.D.F.) responded to the journalist's remark that Anglicanism has always been considered a 'bridge-Church' between Protestantism and Catholicism. 'True,' replied the cardinal prefect, 'but at the moment at least one part of Anglicanism has brusquely distanced itself once again by [its] new norms concerning the re-marriage of divorced persons, the ordination of women, and other questions of moral theology. These are decisions which have re-opened a gap, not only between Anglicans and Catholics, but also between Anglicans and the Orthodox who [in these matters] generally share the Catholic viewpoint'.[5]

Cardinal Ratzinger here manages to suggest that opinion in the Roman Catholic Church is serenely unanimous on all these points. This technique for dealing with theological diversity within the Catholic Church may indeed show members of other Churches where they stand with the Roman Curia, but it does not convey a truthful picture of the variety of Catholic attitudes. All our Churches contain strong elements of inward-looking conservatism, but these elements do not rise to the top with the same apparent inevitability as in the Roman Catholic Church. Internal stresses and strains within any Church have an ecumenical significance, whether or not its members care to admit it.

It is precisely the hesitancy in face of the new directions proposed at Vatican II which exercises Christians of other traditions, as they respond to the insights of the Decree on Ecumenism and the new openness to the Roman Catholic Church to other Churches.

II: AMBIGUOUS PILGRIMAGE

In *Crime and Punishment*, Fyador Dostoyevsky perceptively analyses human motivation and fear. Among the many penetrating insights into human living in the novel is a rhetorical question posed by Rashkolnikov. He muses: 'I wonder, though, what people fear most. It seems to me that what they are afraid of most is taking a new step, or uttering a new word'.[6] The hesitation in the face of the 'new' is a mark of all our histories, corporate and individual. Yet without embracing the 'new' and being susceptible to change there is no possibility of creativity and growth.

Such a period of creativity and growth was undoubtedly heralded at Vatican II not least in the sphere of inter-church relations. The inaugural speech at the council given by Pope John XXIII already signalled the importance of Christian unity in the very conception of the work of the council. The importance of Christian unity for the mission of the Church was anticipated by the creation of a Secretariat for Promoting Christian Unity, and demonstrated by the presence at the council of 'observers' from other Churches, who in fact played a prominent part in the phrasing of the conciliar documents. The council itself then marked a decisive change in relations between the Christian Churches, and suggested how such a change might affect the total life of the Church.

The old policy of isolationism had in fact proved impossible to implement. Biblical, theological and liturgical scholars had in practice been engaged in inter-church specialist gatherings on a variety of themes throughout the century. Indeed without such a dialogue leading to mutual respect it is unlikely that the Second Vatican Council would have been as ecumenically and theologically open as it was. The Second World War had also broken down personal and ecclesial barriers as Protestant, Roman Catholics and Orthodox served together and suffered together[7]. While this was true throughout Europe, any Irish Protestant perception of the situation would have been more nuanced. The breaking down of barriers for him undoubtedly included Roman Catholics, but these were generally English, Scottish or French, not Irish. Of course such a development was regarded by the Vatican as being a matter of human contacts without ecclesiological significance. But since even this was not a shared Irish experience, it left Irish Protestant and Roman Catholic Christians that much less prepared for the event of the Second Vatican Council.

The Second Vatican Council then tried to articulate a new direction for inter-church relations, building on the ecumenical exchanges of this century, by promulgating the Decree on Ecumenism. Significantly, the decree following on the dynamic concept of the Church outlined in the Dogmatic Constitution on the Church describes the movement towards Christian unity as a pilgrimage into the fulness of truth.[8] To undertake such a pilgrimage, of course, involves leaving the safety of the status quo and becoming open to the influences of other pilgrims, as the Way is travelled towards the destination.

By emphasising that the Roman Catholic Church is prepared to undertake the pilgrimage towards Christian unity, the decree discards the notion that Christian unity will only be achieved by all Christian communities returning to the fold of the Roman Catholic Church.[9]

Such a change in terminology from 'return' to 'pilgrimage together towards a fuller understanding of the truth' has not always been grasped by Protestants, including Irish Protestants. That such a change of terminology involved more than a shift in vocabulary tended to lead to Protestants scrutinizing statements and actions for evidence of such change. What was not always perceived by Protestants was that they also had to undergo an equally dramatic ecumenical 'conversion'. Centuries of antagonisms had hardened hearts. Memories of co-operation with Roman Catholics in building their churches and fighting for emancipation had long been replaced by consciousness of *Ne temere*[10], the division of Ireland, and even the memories of families who had come to Ireland in the wake of the revocation of the Edict of Nantes[11]. Even theologically a radical change was needed. Much Protestant theology in Ireland had been conducted in a negative way. We knew a great deal about what we did not believe — usually what was affirmed in Roman Catholic theology[12]. With the change at the Vatican Council not only did Protestants have to rethink Roman Catholic identity; they also had to rethink their own. The old spirit of suspicion and reluctance to change led many in the Irish Churches to read between the lines of the conciliar documents and scent the fragrance of 'return to Rome'.

Of course such a tendency was counterbalanced by the Churches as Churches, who tended to give a much more positive reception to the new openings[13], and many in the Protestant Churches enthusiastically sought better relationships with Roman Catholics through the Glenstal Conference, the Greenhills Conference, membership of the Irish Biblical Association, the Irish Theological Association, and other groupings. Even here, however, the statements and actions of the Roman Catholic Church are still being scrutinized very carefully lest the 'openness' is abandoned.

The call to 'return' was of course always an unrealistic expectation. Besides the hurts caused by the falling out of communion and the antagonisms of centuries of separation, communities grow and develop in the separateness. The Scots poet, Iain Crichton Smith, in his poem 'No Return' reminds us:

No, you cannot return to an island

34

expecting that the dances will be unchanged,
that the currency won't have altered,
that the mountain blue in the evening
will always remain so.
...
Even the boats which you once rowed
have set off elsewhere.[14]

The Roman Catholic Church is not the same as it was in the tenth or the sixteenth centuries. If no changes had occurred in it, it would be a dead body. Neither have the other Christian communities remained unaffected by time, despite the posturings and emotive outbursts at things ecumenical by Protestant fundamentalists who fear a surrender of 'the faith of our fathers' through the very slightest contact with the Roman Catholic Church. However, the centuries of separation have made Protestants hesitant about the change from 'return' to 'pilgrimage', lest the hopes and promises of Vatican II are not fulfilled.

While the Decree on Ecumenism emphasises the idea of pilgrimage, there is equally apparent a hesitancy to abandon a Rome-centred juridical view of the Church as a hierarchical perfect society. This dualism, apparent in the decree itself, has been a constant tension since the council, as we shall see, and it is a tension which continues to cause disquiet, especially among ecumenically orientated Protestants.

The Decree on Ecumenism, while it gave guidelines as to how and why the pilgrimage towards Christian unity needed to be undertaken, was of course not the only ecumenically significant feature of the Second Vatican Council. The presence and activity of 'Observers' gave a clear indication that there was an expectation that the Roman Catholic Church could learn much from the other Christian communities, and expected to do so on the pilgrimage. That the council fathers did in fact so learn is evident in the various documents of Vatican II. The most obvious example of this is the way in which the thought of the Presbyterian New Testament scholar, Oscar Cullmann, is incorporated into the Dogmatic Constitution on Divine Revelation. The ecumenical pilgrimage was further seen to be concerned with every facet of the life and thought of the Church. The pilgrimage was to permeate every aspect of Church life, and was to involve 'the whole Church, faithful and clergy alike', as the Decree on Ecumenism (section 5) notes.

If these then are the fundamental impulses of the council in respect of inter-Church relations, how far in the eyes of Protestants have they dominated the approach by the Roman Catholic Church to other Christian Churches in the past twenty years?

There has certainly been an immense amount of positive ecumenical activity involving the Roman Catholic Church. At the international level, the Vatican has established theological dialogues with nearly every major Christian tradition, showing that it is possible to overcome differences and difficulties and to begin to phrase a common language. This activity at international level has been matched in some areas by the work of national commissions on theological questions being established with the other major traditions in the area[15]. Such work has had an enthusiastic welcome on the whole from Protestants in the 'mainstream' Churches.

However, the dualism of pilgrimage and Rome-centredness is apparent in this theological dialogue up to the present. By participating in dialogues, where the Roman Catholic Church meets one other Christian tradition at a time, there is a danger of the dialogue becoming primarily concerned with the question, 'How like me are you?' Such a question of course is natural in situations where dialogue is being restored after a period where little contact has taken place. In the early days of the Faith and Order movement, where Protestant and Orthodox theologians met to discuss inter-church theological questions, this 'comparative method' of dialogue operated until such a time as theologians from the different Christian theological traditions were in a position to trust each other enough to be able to attempt to do theology together. The 'comparative method'[16] in effect places 'self' at the centre of the ecumenical pilgrimage and finds acceptable only that which images 'self'. This sense of placing 'self' and 'self-understanding' in centre stage is evident also in the response to such inter-church theological dialogue. The comments of the Congregation for the Doctrine of the Faith on the Final Report of the Anglican-Roman Catholic International Commission reinforce, for example, the awareness of the tension between a community on pilgrimage and a Rome-centred ecclesiology, and give great comfort to those Protestants suspicious of Roman Catholic intentions[17].

This 'comparative method' of doing theology has among Protestant and Orthodox churchmen been replaced by a 'cooperative method' where Christians of different traditions together try to articulate a common theology. Such an approach, while it is very evident in the work of the Faith and Order

36

Commission of the World Council of Churches (the Roman Catholic Church is a member of the Commission), is also the approach of the inter-church groups of Irish Protestants. Unfortunately the theological approach in the Ballymascanlon Conversations, where Irish Protestants experience most immediatley the theological dialogue with Roman Catholics, is 'comparative'[18]. There is not a great feeling that there is a preparedness to listen and to change in the light of the insights and experiences of others.

The Decree on Ecumenism and the council's mode of working saw the ecumenical pilgrimage as relating to every facet of life. While there is much ecumenical activity in Ireland and while there is a large number of joint Protestant and Roman Catholic commissions, there has been a tendency to equate 'ecumenism' with 'theological dialogue'[19]. The invitation by the Dublin Council of Churches to the Roman Catholic Archdiocese of Dublin to exploratory talks to form a new and restructured Dublin Council of Churches, with full Roman Catholic participation, led to slightly increased activities between the council and the archdiocese, but the invitation to join the council was rejected. The Diocesan Ecumenical Commission was able only to advise the archdiocese on inter-church theological questions but had no remit in respect of co-operation on issues such as housing, education and unemployment[20]. The ecumenical pilgrimage, however, concerns the whole life of the Christian community. In Ireland especially, Protestants would welcome signs that the Roman Catholic Church is really prepared to work together on social questions and in the sphere of education.

That ecumenism involves the whole life of the Church, and this at congregational level too, is amply illustrated in the guidelines 'Ecumenical Collaboration at the Regional, National and Local Levels'[21], and the large number of shared Protestant and Roman Catholic parishes in England and the increasing number in Scotland[22]. While there is a number of shared churches among the Protestant Churches in Ireland, there are no such shared schemes with Roman Catholic parishes as yet[23]. Other ways, therefore, need to be found to bring congregations together if the radical call to change is to be heeded here.

Despite the impressive amount of ecumenical activity in Ireland, Protestants are still aware that at certain decisive points in Roman Catholic Church life and practice little change has occurred. In the field of theological education, for example, little explicit attention has been paid to the life, thought and practice of other Christian traditions or to inter-church theological approaches[24]. In attitudes towards society, little joint deliberation is evident[25]. These signs of hesitancy are matched by Protestants, who always hesitate to commit themselves wholeheartedly to the ecumenical pilgrimage.

This tendency at times to insist on 'doing one's own thing' seems in turn to be matched by a lack of awareness that any sign of a lack of willingness to listen by the Roman Catholic Church affects Protestant responses. Great hurt occurs, therefore, when the Roman Catholic Church seems to dismiss the views of theologians whose reflections appear to move in the direction of some Protestant and Orthodox ecclesiologies as in the cases of Edward Schillebeeckx, Leonardo Boff and Hans Küng. Disquiet arises at the procedures adopted, and also at what is felt to be a rejection of and lack of openness to a radical questioning on the nature and structure of the Church. Even for the most ecumenically committed Protestants, there is disquiet at such a seeming return to a Rome-centred and controlled ecclesiology.

There can be no doubt that the Second Vatican Council with its Decree on Ecumenism was a decisive event for both Roman Catholics and Christians of other traditions. Relations between the Churches in Ireland will never again revert to a pre-conciliar situation, and an immense amount of positive worth in the restoration of relationships has been achieved in the past twenty years. However, the invitation to pilgrimage for the whole community in every aspect of its life and witness needs to be more courageously embraced, in the light of the human response of hesitancy in the face of the new, as Dostoyevsky so accurately perceived. The council gave an impressive lead. It is time to accept the challenge more determinedly. By so doing the Irish Protestant Churches will also be enabled to overcome their hesitations, and become more committed to the common pilgrimage towards a fuller understanding of the Gospel, and greater commitment to Christian discipleship.

MARGARET MacCURTAIN & NIVARD KINSELLA

Sisters and Brothers

I: SISTERS

One of the recurring themes of the religious paintings of Patrick
Pye is the sacrifice of Abraham. The subject, one of the central
myths on which western civilisation fed, is deeply ambiguous.
The psychological demands made on Abraham by God remind
us powerfully in a world threatened by nuclear holocaust that the
God of history is immanent as well as transcendent. The hidden
God, *Deus absconditus*, leaves us to make our lonely death-filled
decisions, and the God of revelation joyously announces that the
time of testing is over.

For religious men and women in the Irish tradition of religious
life, the divine-human relationship is the great axis on which
religious renewal has moved or remained transfixed. Before the
Second Vatican Council, God for the Irish was outside his world,
splendidly worshipped in the great surging liturgies of Gregorian
chant with their echoes of the life of the world to come, or he was
the God of judgement implacably above the grey skies that
brought the great Famine, who punished as well as rewarded.
Hell and heaven were cosmologically real to those who entered
religious communities in Ireland before the mid-sixties, and the
weekly confession and annual retreat were structures by which
the religious could gauge progress in the 'state of perfection'.

Twenty years after Vatican II, the barometer of renewal is the
realisation by religious communities that they have set out on a
spiritual journey which has changed not only their view of the
cosmos but, awesome feeling, their experience of God. Salvation
history coming from the documents of Vatican II places emphasis on the responsibilities charged to humankind: divine activity
courses through human beings. The world of creation belongs to
God's plan, and we are called to develop it.

How strange to Irish ears in 1965 were the words of paragraph
46 of *The Constitution on the Church*, 1964: 'All men should take
note that the profession of the evangelical counsels, though
entailing the renunciation of certain values which are to be
undoubtedly esteemed, does not detract from a genuine devel-

opment of the human person, but rather by its very nature is most beneficial to that development'.

Ireland's religious orders in the twentieth century were an integral part of the national life of the country and of the Catholic foreign missions. In return, Irish religious orders had been treated generously by appreciative governments north and south. The reliable service of religious in State employment and their pragmatic approach to the country's fragile infra-structure of social welfare and education lay at the heart of their power in Church-State relationships. Paradoxically those same bureaucratic talents were the unguessed-at source of their vulnerability: for unlike their American, or a number of the European co-religionists, Irish religious by and large were immersed in the day-to-day running of their large institutions which they co-partnered with the Irish State and with the Stormont government in Northern Ireland. Human development played a minimal part in novitiate formation in mid-century Ireland, as the literature of the period eloquently demonstrates. In 1965 the Conference of Major Religious Superiors in Ireland was only five years old, and was still in the process of finding a role for itself, beginning to act as an umbrella for the various bodies of religious orders in the country. One of its main tasks was to bring into line the managerial structures of the complex school-systems of the country, technically the greatest power-bloc in Church-State relations, a task still challenging religious renewal twenty years later.

Ready availability of the various council documents in book form came a year later. Over the last twenty years, *Perfectae Caritatis* (the Decree on Renewal of Religious Life) became the most hard-worked document used by religious orders engaged in the daunting task of bringing religious life into line with the council's vision of the place of religious life in its Constitution on the Church. Retrospectively, *Perfectae Caritatis* was a somewhat jejune document setting an impossible target for religious orders in the tension it proposed between tradition and renewal, between recovery of the the spirit of the founder and adaptation to the tempo of the late twentieth century. The seventies with their cycle of successive general chapters faithfully carrying out the agenda laid down in the council's decree left many religious men and women agonizing over the competing claims of western monasticism (strong in the Irish tradition of religious experience) and the call to personhood in the perspective of salvation history. 'Personal fulfilment' became a term of reproach as interim constitutions struggled to free religious communities from the excessive rigidities of timetables, a timeless past, timeless medieval garb, and the accumulation of vocal prayers at set hours. The challenges were overwhelming, and spilled over into liturgical reform, fresh programmes in Christian foundation, contemporary approaches and techniques for the apostolate, ecumenical dialogue, and the more mundane tasks of updating habits and timetables.

From the perspective of 1985 many religious will now admit that it was only in the eighties that Vatican II began to permeate their lives. The 1981 edition of *Vatican II: Conciliar and Post-Conciliar Documents*[1] with their emphasis on accuracy has given, as Cardinal John Wright observed in the preface, 'an air of permanence, completeness, and academic thoroughness'. However, many religious (though not as yet a majority) in Ireland see the Puebla documents from South America as the greatest challenge to Irish religious. There, the openness to social justice, to inner-city renewal, to the rural poor, the move from large convents to small communities associated with the local Church are all now familiar to us as 'the preferential option for the poor'[2]. These documents have afforded some Irish religious a glimpse of what true liberation consists of, and what it means to be 'in dialogue with one's own time'.

But possibly in the context of re-evaluation in the mid-eighties, it is a reflective exercise to work through the list of more important post-conciliar documents appended to the 1981 edition and understand the intensive dialogue going on between the religious orders and the Vatican through the various levels of national and international Unions of Major Superiors, and the various departments of the Vatican during the pontificates of Paul VI, John Paul I, and John Paul II. For the religious seriously engaged in following through the original outline of the Constitution on the Church, the world has become the upside-down Kingdom of the Beatitudes. Unquestioned norms of twenty years ago have been replaced, first by interim directives and draft constitutions and gradually in the eighties by modest constitutions stamped with the approval of the Sacred Congregation for Religious and Secular Institutes. For Irish religious men and women the background to the last twenty years of renewal/reform was struggle: on a personal level to comprehend and encompass the demands on their resources implicit in the Vatican II documents; on a societal level to endeavour to absorb the new theology of religious life even as the political situation in Northern Ireland put Catholics and Protestants into positions that had

41

more to do with the seventeenth century after the Council of Trent than the late twentieth century after Vatican II.

If one asks an Irish religious today to identify the central issue of renewal most meaningful to him or her, the answer varies from the experience of cobbling a new constitution together as chapter delegates, to the crisis of identity around the shedding of a medieval head-dress. Or the answer might instance the adoption of the new vernacular breviary and the application of the 1963 Constitution on the Liturgy, with its challenging post-script of instructions issued mainly in the pontificate of Paul VI, as evidence of the new sap flowing through religious communities. Perhaps because of our historical memory of the eighteenth century Penal Code which suppressed any public display of religious garb or solemnisation of liturgy, Irish religious orders have shown little inclination to take risks with new liturgical forms such as sacred dance and movement, or devising a choir robe that could be used for choral Divine Office, as for example some French religious orders have adopted. We are good at forgetting our spoken roots and we continue to flounder between different musical traditions of hymn-singing, having abandoned the Latin music and Gregorian plain-chant too hastily. Welcome indeed was the the setting-up of the Irish Institute of Pastoral Liturgy in 1974, now based in Carlow, which is making steady inroads on the traditional areas of resistance to outward display. Similarly, Church architects and artists from 1973 onwards have monitored the adaptation of existing chapels, assisting with their advice the construction of chapels, new convents, and prayer-centres. Thus there has been emerging in the last ten years a growing perception among religious of the significance of environment in the proper celebration of the Eucharist, the Divine Office, and other liturgical forms.

There has been, then, on balance more gain than loss in the last twenty years of religious renewal. The revitalisation of spirituality around the charism of the founder has revealed Mary Ward, Catherine McAuley, Ignatius Rice, Nano Nagle, Mary Aikenhead to thousands of religious previously nourished on a thin diet of imported devotions. Scripture and theology! Was there ever so rich a period of learning and scholarship over the last four hundred years as there has been in the twentieth century? Tardily, women theologians and biblical scholars have come on the scene, drawn alike from the laity and women's religious orders. In this field American women scholars in the religious orders have contributed greatly to the Irish sisterhoods.

It has been asserted that women religious in Ireland have been foremost in their endeavour to be formed anew by the decrees of Vatican II. The Focus for Action summer schools and around-the-year workshops in the seventies were among the better init-iatives taken by the C.M.R.S., but the latter's slowness to recog-nise the significance of feminism in Irish society is still a serious block to its dialogue with contemprary forces of change in the country.

One of the most sucessful interventions by the official Irish Church was the setting up in Dundalk in 1969 of the Institute of Religious Education by the bishops of the province of Armagh. It rapidly became a nation-wide centre of pastoral and catech-etical education, Many religious and laity who have experienced its one-year residential diploma course think it is the best exper-ience that has happened them in Ireland since Vatican II, pastor-ally speaking.

For the brotherhoods, both those engaged fully in teaching or health-care, or those brothers in institutes with priest members, renewal has been a complex process. In his visit to Ireland for the centenary celebrations of the St John of God Order, the Prior General warned the Taoiseach that changing times and falling numbers would necessitate retrenchment and rationalisation. There is an even deeper tension which has surfaced as the mean-ing of the brother's vocation has taken on fresh significance for our times. Apart from the categories of canon law, which the new code has not greatly modified, there is a growing realisation that in religious orders the charism is the same, and, for example, in orders where priests and brothers share the apostolate equally, full equality including the office of superior should be accorded in community living.

Any analysis of religious renewal now must take cognisance of the 1983 Code of Canon Law. Some its implications have not yet percolated into the consciousness of religious communities, which have been given, through the code, an acknowledgement of the principles of co-responsibility and subsidiarity to off-set any marked insistence on the authority of religious superiors. There is a temptation, once the constitutions have been drafted and approved by Rome, for religious to feel that the project has been achieved and that they may return to their every-day pre-occupations, leaving chapters and major superiors to do their thinking for them. There seems to be an inbuilt resistance in religious to *process*. Joseph Dargan, S.J., in his presidential address to the C.M.R.S. says: 'For us, *process* is all important,

43

No matter what policy we develop at the present time, it will be out of date in three years time. That is why we need to be able to learn to reflect on our experience, to make decisions, to take action and not to be afraid to evaluate this action, and change it when necessary'[3].

Irish history and the nature of Church-State relationships in the twentieth century have conditioned us to a work-filled life. There exists the persistent idea in our society that religious, especially the non-clerical groups, brothers and sisters, exist to perform tasks determined not only by their institutes but by the State. For many Irish people, service — and by implication one's self-definition in terms of work — are still all-important. Visitors to Ireland remark frequently that 'What are you doing?' is a much more familiar question than 'Who are you?' Commenting on Canon 573 of the new code, ('life consecrated through profession of the evangelical counsels is a stable form of living') Jerome Murphy-O'Connor, O.P., writes: 'We appear to be confronted with the concept of "state of perfection" which was consciously abandoned by Vatican II'[4]. In status-conscious Ireland of the 'eighties, where class is determined by income[5], there is a real danger that religious will once again be pulled into the workaholic syndrome. The Jesuit psychiatrist Angelo d'Agostino puts the 'state of perfection' mentality into context: 'The good religious of pre-Vatican II days were those who were predictably consistent. They kept the same schedule every day of their religious life. They repeated the same prayers at the same time and in the same manner every day. This was the usual criterion on which we based our judgement of the good religious. In the post-Vatican II Church the position is reversed. Good religious are those who are flexible and adaptable. They are no longer those who are rigid in adhering to constancy but rather those who can meet the constantly changing realities of life them'[6].

No review of religious renewal in Ireland in the last twenty years is complete without acknowledging the presence of the Women's Movement in Ireland during the same period. The Women's Movement has emerged as a powerful agent of social and political change, and in the 'eighties, is beginning to attract in a serious way the commitment of a small but ever-increasing number of religious women in the country. Progress on women's issues since the 'sixties has involved women's groups and organisations. By the 'eighties networks have been set up around social problems such as rape, domestic violence, health-care and childcare. There have been initiatives in feminist journalism and publishing, in research, literature, music, biblical and theological studies. Feminist spirituality in Dublin has attracted hundreds of women, including women religious. On a global scale the emergence of women as a critical force in a number of crucial struggles facing humanity has been a key-development. From Selma to South Africa, women religious have witnessed to justice side by side with their lay sisters and brothers.

There are clear challenges to women in religious orders in Ireland in this present decade. These include new peace interventions in Northern Ireland, active participation in nuclear disarmament programmes, more involvement in ecumenical dialogue, and the assumption of leadership in areas which involve the reaching out to the powerless at this crucial period of history. On a negative note, the relationship of Irish women religious with the Irish hierarchy has been cordial if muted: they are rarely invited to participate at episcopal conferences, or have their views carried to the synods at Rome.

There is a feeling of anti-climax about the mid-eighties in Ireland despite the gains of the last twenty years. The euphoric atmosphere which accompanied the introduction of the new constitutions has disappeared, while the scarcity of vocations and ageing membership lend a certain air of hesitation to the way forward. One clear element has run consistently through the renewal programmes over the years since Vatican II closed in 1965: it is important for bishops, laity and for religious themselves not to define religious primarily by what they do. There is a quiet acceptance now that the time is approaching for religious to sever their institutional identity from schools and hospitals. Pope John Paul II has stated his conviction that 'apostolically, the presence of religious women in a local Church is more important than that of a priest'[7].

For male religious in Ireland collaboration with the hierarchy in meeting the urgent needs of new parishes has been the most visible feature of the last decade. Again, in speaking to major religious superiors of men in 1983, Pope John Paul II described the Church of today as 'the community of disciples'. It is a particularly felicitous description for the Irish Church to hearken to, for the Irish Church traces its origins back to St Patrick. Patrick, it has been said, 'established a Church in perfect conformity with the spirituality of the place'[8]. The secret of Patrick's effective evangelisation was his willingness to accept the indigenous traditions, and to adapt his message to them.

There is an urgency demanded of religious in Ireland today —
many past their first prime — to discover the contemporary
values, customs, traditions of our society. Now is a time of
youthfulness in our country and also, tangibly, of mellow old
age. We need to retrieve Patrick's sense of ecology, to regain the
spiritual talent of being soul-friends, *anam-chairde*, to young and
old, and to turn our institutional convents into centres where
people will find spirituality and kinship. Our *kenosis*, or
emptying-out, as religious, consists of shedding extreme forms of
nationalism and xenophobia, of eliminating sectarian viruses
from our Catholic Christianity, and of reconciling the warring
traditions on this island. The call, like that which Patrick heard,
is again the distressed voice of the Irish inviting the authentic
evangelist to come and live among them.

II: BROTHERS

In the 1950s the religious of Ireland were riding high on a wave of
large numbers, full novitiates, and an apparently ever-expanding
future. The winds of change were as yet only a mild and gentle
breeze. The cloud was already on the horizon, but it was still no
bigger than a man's hand. The solid piety and devotion of the
people seemed to ensure that nothing would ever change.

If you read the religious magazines and newspapers of the day
you will find nothing in them about the need for change in the
Church. Perhaps some religious, who had received their training
in continental Europe, had heard about this, but, if they had,
they kept it to themselves. The experience of the war had largely
passed Ireland by. Our stand on neutrality, however admirable,
had served to reinforce us in the idea that somehow we were
slightly superior to others.

We were Catholic, and we liked to recall that this meant being
uncritically Roman. The country was largely homogeneous,
mainly rural, solidly Roman Catholic and in the main unaware of
impending social change.

Religious life was a high and noble ideal, constantly proposed
to young men and women, and responded to with generosity and
enthusiasm. The theology of the religious life was clear and
certain, and religious generally saw themselves as superior to the
laity. No one said that *only* religious were called to holiness, but
neither did they say that there was one universal call. Religious
admitted that lay people *could* become holy, but the religious
was holy by virtue of his state.

46

Then came the Council, and while its decrees have affected the lives of religious in many ways, I think one item can be singled out as the pebble bouncing down the mountainside. This was chapter five of the Constitution on the Church, 'The Call to Holiness'. Other sections of the council's decrees had wider impact later on, and led to more far-reaching changes, e.g., in the liturgy. But this was not evident at the time, and nothing in *Perfectae Caritatis*, the decree on religious life, matched the profundity of this chapter. The idea that there is *one* call to holiness in the Church shook many religious. The words of the chapter, 'It is *quite clear that all Christians in any state or walk of life* are called to the fulness of Christian life and the perfection of love', sounded somewhat like an alarm bell. For they said that everyone is called to holiness, by virtue of their Baptism. You did not have to be a religious to become holy. No matter what your vocation in the Church, your call to holiness is rooted in your being a Christian rather than in the religious state. In its way this one chapter was more important than the whole decree on religious life. It found echoes in the deep subconscious doubts that many religious had always had about where precisely holiness is to be found.

But the council and *Lumen gentium* were not the only agents for change, affecting religious life as they did the wider world of the 1960s. Two factors peculiar to the Irish situation may be noted. One of these was the belated arrival of economic planning under Seán Lemass and T. K. Whitaker: the national transformation which this effected, inevitably affected the life of the Church as a whole. But it also brought the *idea* of planning as a science even into religious communities, who had long subsisted on the principle that God would provide.

Television came to Ireland at about the same time and it spelt the end of our isolation as a nation. The world was no longer 'out there'. It was in our living rooms. It soon became apparent that censorship could no longer work. From being insular, and unexposed to the cultural diversity and richness of other lands and peoples, we were suddenly open to the world.

Where censorship and the law had supported Christian values, the satellite and the T.V. aerial might end them. For the first time, whether for good or ill, we had entered an open society. Nor could initial restrictive reaction on the part of authority exclude religious from this.

And there was a third factor of world-wide significance. Possibly the profoundest effect of the two great wars of this century has been the 'authority crisis'. So many died, and so many died pointlessly ... It slowly dawned on the world that too much authority was simply power, and too much of it was misused, as in the Holocaust and the wars, and later in Vietnam and Watergate. All this has led to a great mistrust of all authority, not excluding the Church, seen by so many as simply another authoritarian organisation. Within it, the religious orders, with their vows of obedience, are seen as the very epitome of this authoritarian attitude, and those in them as being unquestioning and passive to a degree that is not acceptable to people today.

This attitude has also led many religious to question much of the tradition in religious life, and there is a widespread mistrust of authority evident among religious today. While no doubt there are excesses in this regard, this has been a good development, and has led in part to the current stress on personal development as *the* essential part of formation, with its accompanying emphasis on the need for personal responsibility and decision.

THE FALL IN VOCATIONS

The drop in the number of those entering religious life did not come until the mid-sixties, after the council had ended. It was probably due partly to the council itself, and to some loss of confidence in their vocation by religious themselves; to the emergence of a spirituality of affirmation after the council, against which the classic spirituality of religious life seemed outdated and passé; to the number of priests and religious who left at that time. While we did not suffer as some other countries did, a fair number did go. Tables 1 and 2 set out some of the facts.[9]

Table 1

	1970	1984	
Numbers			
Clerical religious	7858	6620	15% decrease
Brothers	2537	1643	32% decrease
Entrants			
Clerical religious	252	98	
Brothers	187	27	

Among clerical religious 35% of the decrease was due to deaths, 65% due to departures; among brothers, 27% was due to deaths, 73% due to departures.

48

	Table 2
Age level	
Clerical religious	In 1970 11% were over 60 years of age
	In 1981 this had risen to 27%
Brothers	In 1970 11% were over 60 years of age
	in 1981 this had risen to just under 20%

It is clear that the proportion of those over sixty will increase rapidly as the age level rises, with consequent deaths and retirements from active work increasing. What is most worrying is that more men are leaving than are dying, and the number of those leaving is *still* proportionately high. Thus in 1984, 96 clerical religious died and 122 departed; that same year 30 brothers died and 44 departed. Comparable figures in 1971 were 79 deaths and 169 departures among clerical religious, with 34 deaths and 159 departures among the brothers. (The figure for departures includes novices.)

It is only now that the drop in vocations is having an effect. And it is only now that we are facing the fact that this is not so much a vocations crisis (something which will end soon) as the beginning of a new erea in the Irish Church. This will be characterised by a much wider sharing by laity in the ministry, and by the increasing involvement of the people at all levels.

Is it possible that some religious orders will disappear? Possibly some will effectively disappear through amalgamation, but one of the more remarkable phenomena during the recent past has been the impact of the smaller groups. Size is not a guarantee of effectiveness nor of permanence. The groups that have made most impact seem to have concentrated on forming their men precisely to be facilitators and animators, or else have worked with highly professional lay men and have concentrated on forming a team with them. But it is certain that some congregations will get smaller. This holds for the monasteries of monks and very likely for some of the missionary congregations. The numbers in the monasteries of men have gone down by about fifty (15%) in the past two decades. More important is the very high age level of the communities now, which averages over sixty, and the fact that the number entering some of the abbeys has dropped to zero for several years.

With the changing pattern of work in the developing countries

49

the missionary congregations are facing a new challenge. The rise of the lay missionary movement, as well as the reluctance of some governments to allow missionaries into their territories without problematic conditions, make the task more difficult and a lot less clear than it was. But the backing these congregations are giving to the lay missionaries, and their use of these men and women with a short-term commitment, is a sign of their vitality, and a sign of hope for the future. Like so much else, it points to a *different* kind of Church. The big seminary buildings will go, if they have not gone already, and the amalgamation of training facilities points to survival.

THE PARISH

Since 1970 a decline in the numbers of diocesan clergy, a population increase of almost half a million, and the growth of large centres, notably Dublin, have put increased pressure on the parish system. The number of parishes has increased by about 140, and this has made it inevitable that religious would have to move into parochial work. Many religious have taken over parishes, both in the older city areas and in the newer developing housing estates at the edge of the cities.

At first after an initial welcome, lack of mobility and flexibility in the apostolate led to much heart-searching by religious. This attitude is now changing, and there is an increasing awareness among religious that the move has been providential, that they have a distinctive contribution to make to the parish apostolate precisely as religious.

The results of this new thinking can be seen in team ministry, in the involvement of all the religious in the parish, including parish sisters, and of the laity. This is not to suggest that it is only in religious parishes that this happens, but it is a fact that religious men have shown a readiness to work with women, whether religious or lay, which is surprising given their background and formation. One reason for this readiness to engage in new ventures is probably what can be called the 'chapter mentality'. Religious are used to working in community, and to taking part in chapter discussions. Their formation enables them to pool ideas and share responsibility for the apostolate.

EVANGELISATION

The documents from the holy see and the synod of bishops in the past decade have been among the most important post-conciliar statements to appear. Coupled with the theology in these has

50

been the experience, new to Ireland, of meeting the 'de-churched' in large numbers. This has led to a re-think on the part of the whole Church as to what evangelisation means. There is a growing mistrust of counting heads as a way of counting Christians. The emergence of a 'theology of non-practice/disbelief', the work of Irish theologians who are using the research done in other countries, allied to their own experience here, is of the greatest importance.

Another aspect of this is the option for the poor showing itself in the move to the inner city by groups of men religious. This is not entirely new, as we have always had the large city centre churches run by the religious orders. The difference in the new approach is that the apostolate with the people is not tied to the church. The religious community itself is the means of evangel-isation, and community life shared with the local people is an important part of it. This practice is not yet widespread among men religious, but it is happening. No doubt the women religious can do it better as they can get nearer the families in the homes. But the men are needed too. Liberation theology Irish style? Perhaps. Certainly, it is filling a need and taking the Gospel to where the people are which is not in the churches.

C.M.R.S.

The Conference of Major Religious Superiors was set up in 1961. For some years it was a loosely-knit group meeting periodically to talk about common problems and ways of co-operating. Religious orders in Ireland have always been somewhat stand-offish with each other, even when working in the same area of the city or the same field of the apostolate. In 1974 Fr Cecil McGarry, then Provincial of the Jesuits, and President of the Conference, invited a group of people to form what later becoem known as the Focus for Action working party. This group produced a report, on the state of religious life in Ireland, made some projections about the future ten years, and some suggestions about the challenges that lay ahead. (At the same time the conference itself was re-organised with a permanent secretary general, an elected president and executive).

It was clear at that time that the clouds were gathering, and the Focus for Action Report appealed to religious to prepare people for the storms ahead about abortion, divorce, and other moral issues. Its predictions have in fact been borne out by events, although some of its recommendations (e.g. about adult educ-ation as a priority), are only now being taken up in some dioc-

51

eses. The whole emphasis was only partly successful, but it was the first instance of religious of different orders getting together with lay people and others in a united effort.

The Focus group saw renewal through education and personal development as the key to success and produced a plan for putting every religious in the country through this renewal over a five-year period. Some applauded, and took it up eagerly; some ignored it, and some remained unconvinced. In general, the women were more eager in their resposne than the men, and, in fact, co-operation between men and women was one of the positive results of the project.

SOCIAL JUSTICE

With the increasing exposure of religious to new ideas came a new development. A conviction took hold that preaching the Gospel necessarily means preaching justice, and looking hard at society and its structures. This has led to a stress on the need for social analysis, which is now part of the preparation for chapter of many religious. The C.M.R.S. has set up the 'justice desk', with a permanent staff, and the conscientisation which has follow ed may prove to be one of the most far-reaching decisions of the conference.

Again, religious men have not got involved in the social apostolate as much at women, but they are realising its importance more and more. The move to the inner city, the Report on the Travelling People, the Companions for Justice, and in general the increasing readiness of religious to acquaint themselves at first hand with the poverty of the very poor, all indicate this heightened awareness. So does a growing stress in current religious writing on the need for the reformation of unjust structures in society. The prophetic word seems to be emerging again ...

SHARING FORMATION

Since Vatican II the big shift in formation has been from training people for jobs to forming them as persons. This is an enormous shift of focus, and religious have come to realise that no one congregation can go it alone any longer. The foundation of the Milltown Institute and the sharing of formation courses for young religious point this up. Most significant of all, the C.M.R.S. has established a house of formation for the purpose of training those of both sexes responsible for formation in their respective congregations. There is also a course stretching over several summers available at the Milltown Institute for the same purpose.

In all this the emphasis is on personal development, without which one meets with resistance to change from people who feel threatened by it or who see no need for it. Inter-congregational dependency has become a reality: more and more we are convinced that, unless we work together, resources will be squandered and results will be the poorer.

We have mentioned the shift in the formation model from the functional to the anthropological. In a recent remarkable address to the C.M.R.S. Sister Patricia Sweeney had the following to say: 'Today we are being called to expand our vision of formation — to take the emphasis off the formation of religious and direct it to the formation of Christians, of communities of Christians ... the real challenge is to provide a Christian formation that addresses the whole people as community of Christians, providing an opportunity for all to grow spiritually together, that all may be involved effectively in ministry — this is the real challenge'[10]. Sister Sweeney headed the new Institute of Formation in its first three years.

Among the most necessary resources for formation and the deepening of commitment is the provision of literature which is current, professional, and Irish. Otherwise we depend on input from other countries, and admirable though this be, it is not in touch with the Irish scene. Here we must pay tribute to Austin Flannery, O.P., under whose direction Dominican Publications has filled this need admirably with *Religious Life Review* and a continual stream of books about the religious life and the problems facing the Irish Church. His *Conciliar and Post-Conciliar Documents* has become the standard text, and it is one of the success stories of the Irish religious scene in the last two decades.

THE FAILURES

But not all has been success. There are still too many male religious who have never been exposed to any sort of renewal, since the council, or indeed since their final profession. On any renewal course what stands out is the small number of men present and the large number of sisters. This can be partly explained by the fact that there are many more sisters than men religious in Ireland — 14,228 against 6,620, so the proportion is just over two to one. But the proportion of women to men on courses is often nine or ten to one! The 'training syndrome' comes into this. Religious priests have been trained for years in theology, and taught to have clear and definite answers to, e.g., moral problems. Religious brothers are, in the main, teachers, also highly trained and sure of their subject. Both have the occupational hazard of thinking that they know all the answers. Many of them in fact come to believe this! So what is the need to go on courses and learn it all again? (And, of course, *all* Irish males know all the answers — while being singularly reluctant to face themselves and their own emotions.)

There are other factors which come into it: recreation patterns, reactions against 'too much' community living and 'too much' formation, and so on. So excellent opportunities are often unavailed of, and many of our men religious have been untouched by any theological or personal renewal.

One of our major failures has surely been that we have not moved forward in education as we might have. The day of amalgamation, lay principals, co-education, and smaller religious presence in the schools is with us, and has been for some time. It had been predicted for longer still. Remember the F.I.R.E. Report? That was well before Focus. It got little publicity, partly because we were afraid of publicity then, and partly because we did not know how to deal with the unions. How many religious have sent men for training in labour relations? Or on management courses? We are still not at ease in the world of negotiation, bargaining, and redundancies. But this is the real world of today and we must get into it, with as much skill as we can muster. We could have moved from a position of strength long ago, but we failed because we were afraid.

We also failed in that we have taken the values of our middle class which are worthy, good and upright but not particularly prophetic or evangelical. We have not been different. Indeed since the time of the founders, most of us have not been creative, and thus we have failed to produce a positive Catholic policy for our schools. So we see the young men who have been in them for six years, leave and drift away from the faith.

Brother Jerome Kiely, F.P.M., one of the most experienced educationalists in the country, has had this to say: 'We are facing a crisis in our schools ... we have three options: either to leave it as it is, or to continue to patch it up, or to replace the system with a new one ... I propose that we grasp the opportunity of the present crisis ... '[11] Brother Jerome would not be talking like that if we had not failed already.

We have also failed to use the media for evangelisation as we might have. This is a criticism of the Church in Ireland in general and perhaps the religious could not have given the lead in the matter. Anyhow, they didn't. Perhaps we need a 'media desk' in the C.M.R.S. along with the others.

One reason why we have not had more conspicuous failures may be that we have not experimented enough. Most of the ventures we have undertaken have been safe ones, and they have worked out well. Perhaps in view of the charism of being religious we should experiment more. For the role of the religious is prophetic, and this means being open to new needs and new opportunities in the Church and society. It is not the function of religious just to keep the system going or to prop up existing institutions. In the words of that most prophetic of men, Pope John XXIII: 'The past will never return. New situations demand new provisions'.[12]

CÉLINE MANGAN, O.P.

The Book and the People

'The documents which have already been promulgated by the Vatican Council have laid great stress on Sacred Scripture, and the reformed liturgy will acquaint both clergy and faithful with sections of the Bible which have hitherto been unfamiliar. As a consequence, priests are looking for guidance in understanding the scriptural foundation for the new trends in doctrine and they want help in the preparation of scriptural homilies. Scripture readings in the vernacular have already stimulated the laity to put questions to priests who do not always feel equipped to answer them. Retreat and mission preachers must give a biblical slant to their preaching if they are to make their indispensable contribution to the realisation of the ideals of the Vatican Council. In novitiates and seminaries students must be taught to nourish their spiritual life on biblical and liturgical sources. In the schools boys and girls will make increasing demands on the staff as new Scripture passages are read to them each day at Mass'.

To some this quotation will sound quite passé; others might well nod their heads in agreement. It is in fact the opening paragraph of an address given by the then Fr Dermot Ryan to the Conference of Major Religious Superiors of Ireland on 22 April 1965.[1] Looking back, it will be possible to say that at least some of the aspirations outlined in that address have been fulfilled. And most people will acknowledge the significant contribution made by the journal *Scripture in Church*, founded by Austin Flannery, in collaboration with Martin McNamara.

In an article entitled, 'The Bible in Irish Spirituality'[2] Martin McNamara, M.S.C., points out that the formative period of Irish Christianity is a model for our use of Scripture today. The early Irish Church had a great love of sacred Scripture as a gift of God to build up the Church in confidence and unity. They appreciated the need for serious study of Scripture. And the Celtic Church proclaimed the necessity of 'preaching the word of God (*procept brethrí Dé*) to the faithful out of the holy Scripture.' (From the *Leabhar Breac*). These three areas of concern to the early Irish Church are also what the Constitution on Revelation called us to

56

at the time of Vatican II. Perhaps they could provide a jumping-off ground, therefore, to see how we have really fared as regards the use of Scripture among the people in the past twenty years.

LOVE OF SCRIPTURE

An immediate reaction here, I think, would be to say, 'We're nowhere near that!' And of course that's true. Twenty years is a short time in the changing patterns of spirituality, and many of us were brought up with at least the suspicion that the Bible was a Protestant book. Old traditions die hard. But there have been giant strides too. I think in particular of the scriptural basis given to the new catechetical programme for primary schools, *The Children of God* series. When I recently heard a six-year-old say, 'Isn't God wonderful!' rather than 'God is out to get me', I realised that we have not yet reaped the benefits of this programme among the adult population.

One sector within the Irish Church in particular which has really taken the scriptural renewal to heart is the sisterhood. The members of the various orders of sisters in Ireland have been diligent in updating their own knowledge of Scripture, and have very quickly made it part and parcel of their spirituality. We have only to compare religious life just before and immediately after the council to see how the words of Dermot Ryan quoted at the beginning have been realised: 'in novitiates and seminaries students must be taught to nourish their spiritual life on biblical and liturgical sources.' Sisters have expected also (and largely obtained) that 'retreat and mission preachers must give a biblical slant to their preaching ...' Now that more and more sisters are involved in retreat work themselves, this is even more true.

I think it is no accident either that it is from among the sisters that the most vibrant call to social reform has been heard in the Irish Church. As Olivia O'Leary has pointed out (*The Sunday Tribune*, 28 July 1985) in relation to the growing involvement of the Church in questions of social concern: 'I think that this could be one of the most important changes in Irish political life in the next few years, especially as the Church is such an enormous channel of communication in this country. And it's also very interesting to see that it's the women, the nuns, who are the more radicalised element at the moment. They'll change things in a peculiarly Irish way, applying Irish terms to an Irish solution, until something is worked out'. Whatever about the 'Irish solution', the conscientisation of the sisters is as much due to their reading of the Scriptures in a radical way as it is to their work on

57

the ground among the poor and deprived both at home and abroad.

The charismatic renewal movement too has opened up the Scriptures for many in Irleand, giving them a new appreciation of faith in Jesus Christ and the realisation of the power of his Spirit. There has been an ecumenical aspect to this renewal which has seen Christians of all denominations sharing what they have in common, precisely in the Scriptures. True, there have been weaknesses in the movement's use of the Bible, and consequently the leadership at the moment are keenly aware of the need for sound teaching. This is especially necessary in view of the tendency towards fundamentalism which can be present within groups. This can take two forms: a Catholic fundamentalism which falls back again into the old superstitious pieties from which the council rightly sought to release us; and a Protestant fundamentalism, characteristic of American Bible-belt evangelism, which takes a material interpretation of Scripture and applies it literally to today's events. While the former takes the call to renewal and familiarises it again in the comfortable old moulds, the latter seems to be a call to conversion but is often really no more that a packaged inoculation against true renewal. All the mainline Churches, north and south of the border, are at the moment experiencing a fall-off in membership towards these fundamentalist groups. Some of these are set up as house-churches based strictly on Scripture; others are more traditional Bible-belt type evangelical groups.

THE SERIOUS STUDY OF SCRIPTURE

At one level this area rates as one of the greatest successes in the application of *Dei Verbum* in the Irish Church. Most bishops and major superiors have been diligent in sending personnel to train in Scripture studies: to the Gregorian in Rome, the École Biblique in Jerusalem, Tübingen, and other centres. At home, the quality of Scripture training in places like Maynooth, the Milltown Institute, and the various seminaries and houses of study has been very high. The academic level of Scripture study has certainly been taken seriously by the Irish Catholic Church, and the availability of the Semitic langauges course in University College, Dublin, has provided a good foundation for biblical studies for many over the years.

A forum for people in the field for the past twenty years has been the Irish Biblical Association (I.B.A.). At the time of its foundation under the leadership of Monsignor Boylan, the title was the 'Catholic Biblical Association of Ireland'. But it very quickly became evident that it could also provide a forum for academic work among Protestant scholars too, and thus the name was changed to simply the 'Irish Biblical Association'. Its purpose is to promote scientific study of the Bible, to support the publication of such studies, to organise conferences and lectures on biblical topics, and to assist the Irish Church in its work of understanding and proclaiming the word of God. In recent years we have seen the appearance of *An Bíobla Naofa*, edited by Pádraig Ó Fiannachta of Maynooth, a project in which many members of the association were involved as they are at the moment on the forthcoming Irish biblical-theological dictionary, to be edited by Martin McNamara, M.S.C. Fr McNamara has been one of the giants in biblical scholarship in Ireland in the past twenty years. Not only has he been active in early Irish Scripture studies, but also, with Kevin Cathcart and Michael Maher, he is at present editing an English-language version of the Aramaic Bible. As a result of his efforts, Dublin has become an important centre of targumic studies. At a more popular level, Fr McNamara was also one of the editors of the *Old Testament Message* series, while the New Testament counterpart of that series had another great name in Irish biblical scholarship at the editorial helm, Fr Wilfrid Harrington, O.P. Fr Harrington's books since the council have more than any others opened up the Bible to lay readership in Ireland.

In Ireland the biblical academic scene is very different to its counterparts in the U.S.A. or on the continent. With the exception of those in the universities, most of those involved in academic work are also active pastorally, fulfilling the other function of the I.B.A.: 'to assist the Irish Church in its work of understanding and proclaiming the word of God.' There have been many calls on the members of the I.B.A. to help in running Scripture courses the length and breadth of the country, and these have been answered generously: Sunday evening Lenten programmes in Ballyshannon, Co. Donegal; Tuesday night in-service theological courses in Carlow; Thursday evening renewal programmes in Mullingar ... the list in the files is endless, and the same few names keep recurring again and again. This kind of work did not leave much time for serious academic work in Ireland, and the miracle is that any got done at all in the past twenty years. It is possible that the next twenty will see a split between the academic and the pastoral fields. If they do, there will indeed be gains, but, I suspect, some losses as well.

In post-primary schools there have indeed been many gains but some losses also. Vatican II caught many secondary teachers, religious and lay, 'on the hop'. As with the training needed in seminaries, the bishops and major superiors were again quick to respond: Mater Dei in Dublin, Mount Oliver in Dundalk, the catechetical course in University College, Dublin, and the opening up of the B.D. course in Maynooth — all came into being promptly. So also the commissioning of new programmes, for example, the *God and Man* series, one volume of which (Bríd Greville's *According to Your Word*) was an approach to Scripture worked out especially for teenagers. These programmes, however, did not have the same far-reaching appeal or results as the excellent primary school series. It took longer for the new training programmes to take effect in secondary schools, and for some time after the council there was a vacuum in religious education from which the schools are only now recovering. The questions were harder to answer, as Dr Ryan had pointed out in 1965: 'In the schools boys and girls will make increasing demands on the staff as new Scripture passages are read to them each day at Mass'. But what is at stake is not just Scripture passages 'read to them each day at Mass' (do they even hear them on Sundays?) but the whole basis of Scripture in their lives, and even religion itself. As we shall see, the whole approach to Scripture needs to be re-examined. Recent surveys have shown the lack of interest and appeal of religion as a subject to post-primary school pupils. See, for example, Dr Ann Breslin's 'A Survey of Senior Students' Attitudes towards Religion, Morality, Education'.[3]

Some have thought that the answer lies in making religion an examination subject on a par with other examination subjects, as is done for the O and A level examinations in Northern Ireland. The religion papers in these examinations are strongly based on Scripture as being an area of religion common to all the denominations there. A syllabus for the Leaving Certificate was actually compiled and completed in 1981, but it has remained at the blueprint stage ever since, largely for technical reasons, but also because there is much opposition to the idea of making religion an examination subject at all. That syllabus also was strongly scriptural in character. A possible approach to the teaching of religion in schools is being tried to some extent in a few schools at present: to treat religion as an academic subject, imparting information on it geared to level of attainment of the age-group involved, while at the same time having a chaplaincy service in the school which would be apart from the actual teaching.

So much for Scripture at the teaching level. How about the rank and file of adults in the Church? As has been suggested already, there has been a great demand for instruction in biblical matters in some quarters, and efforts have been made to meet that demand. Already by 1964, Dermot Ryan was providing courses at the Dublin Institute of Adult Education. These have developed in parishes all over Dublin, and under the auspices of the Maynooth Adult Education Programme very successful two-year courses have been organised all over the country. St Mary's College of Education in Belfast has also been a centre for the provision of such courses. A recent course which deserves special mention is the Diploma in Biblical and Theological Studies in Trinity College, Dublin. Inaugurated by Dr Seán Freyne when he was appointed to the chair of biblical studies there, it fills a gap left by the lack of theological and biblical studies in general at the colleges of the National University other than Maynooth. To my mind, the absence of an educated Catholic laity who would have a theological training behind them from university days, is one of the greatest lacks in the Irish Church at the present time.

PREACHING OUT OF HOLY SCRIPTURE
Activity there has been aplenty, therefore, in the Irish Church of the past twenty years. But has it all added up to a 'great love of sacred Scripture as a gift of God to build up the Church in confidence and unity'? I am afraid the answer would have to be that it has not. We have fallen down, I think, precisely at the level of 'preaching ... *out* of holy Scripture'. Those of us in the front line of biblical studies may have been so busy helping people to know *about* the Scriptures that we failed to go on from there to be concerned enough about the faithful at large. Perhaps a concerted action of scriptural and liturgical reform could have been undertaken. It certainly was not forthcoming, and what effort was made was largely done at a private level by individual Scripture scholars or groups. It is interesting that Dermot Ryan was involved in such efforts at an individual and group level before becoming Archbishop of Dublin, but he did not seem to see it as a priority once he became involved in the traumas of administering one of the biggest dioceses in the world.

Perhaps this is precisely one of the weaknesses of the Irish hierarchy: they have had too many other demands on their psyches in the past twenty years to give priority to the demand of *Dei Verbum*: 'It is for bishops 'with whom the apostolic doctrine resides' suitably to instruct the faithful entrusted to them in the correct use of the divine books ... ' (cf. paragraph 25)

There was no pastoral, for example, from the Irish bishops on the use of Scripture among the faithful, and the excellent pastorals which we did have were sometimes marred by a use of Scripture which was not always sensitive to up-to-date biblical research on modern issues. To take the latest pastoral, *Love is for Life* (1985) as an example, there are many instances where the use of Scripture is not only insensitive but also actually faulty. On page 22, to take but one example, we have:"Great saints have fallen into sins of the flesh. We need only recall St Mary Magdalen and St Augustine. Magdalen, *a notorious public sinner*, [italics mine] became one of the first to meet the Risen Lord and was chosen as one of the first heralds of the resurrection. 'Many sins (were) forgiven her,' the Lord said, 'because she loved much' (Cf. Luke 7:36-50)" Whatever about St Augustine, *nowhere* in the New Testament is it said that Mary Magdalen was a *sinful woman*, not to mention a 'notorious public sinner'. And the texts of the *Prayer of the Church* for her feastday are very careful not to perpetuate this misconception. The misconception arose because of the juxtaposition of the text quoted above (Luke 7:47) — which speaks of an *unnamed* sinful woman — with Mary Magdalen mentioned in Luke 8:2 where it is said of her, 'from whom seven devils had gone out'. But nowhere in the Gospels is the driving out of devils linked with disordered sexuality. Rather it is usually associated with illnesses. I am commenting on this passage at some length because to my mind it shows up much of the weakness in the approach to Scripture of the Irish hierarchy since the council. True, the bishops and others in authority were zealous in providing sound experts in Scripture in accordance with the norm. But they themselves made insufficient use of the findings of their experts in preparing pastoral documents or in working out pastoral programmes. The bishops' Theological Commission, for example, on which members of the I.B.A. serve, could have been of some use to the bishops themselves in preparing for the forthcoming Extraordinary Synod of Bishops in Rome, but offers of help for this preparation were graciously declined.

For whatever reason, and the bishops cannot take all the blame, the use of Scripture in the liturgy in particular (cf. Constitution on Revelation, 24) has probably been the weakest development in the Irish Church since the council. We have largely failed, I think, in the hermeneutical circle: we have not brought the book of life into life for the living Church.

But there are fresh signs of new life burgeoning at present, signs of life from which all of those who are professionals in the field can learn. For example, the first into the field in adult education, the Dublin Institute of Adult Education, has recently changed its approach to Scripture groups. Learning from basic Christian communities in Latin America and elsewhere, it sees itself as no longer providing the 'expert' with all the answers, but a 'facilitator' who helps the group to open up the Scriptures for itself. There are many other similar groups springing up especially in Dublin, and other groupings, such as the Focolare, the Young Christian Workers, the Taizé prayer groups, seek to bring the Bible into life for those who belong to them. Groups like these need to be encouraged and fostered not least because they are a counter-balance to the sects and house-churches mentioned earlier which are sweeping the country. Maybe these groups are the green shoots which are the result of the laborious sowing of the seed these past twenty years. All is not lost.

CONCLUSION

It seems to me that the following are specific areas of concern about the Scriptures for the Church in Ireland for the immediate future:

a) An honest examination by exegetes of problem areas in the Church which have a basis in Scripture: e.g. violence; women and the Church; ministries within the Church; divorce.

b) A genuine fostering and encouragement — rather than mere toleration — of Scripture groups that have an orientation to life rather than being merely academic. At the same time, there is a continuing need for the provision of good teaching about the Bible at all levels.

c) A more active exploration of the media in the presentation of the message of Scripture.

d) A continuation of social analysis in Ireland in the light of the Gospel, work pioneered by the Conference of Major Religious Superiors' Justice Office, and the Jesuit Centre of Faith and Justice.

LOUIS McREDMOND

Sweet Liberty

Irish influence brought about a development of doctrine by the
Second Vatican Council of special relevance to the modern
world. It was a delayed-action influence for it came, not from the
Irish bishops at the council, but from the Catholic Irish of one
hundred and forty years ago, a people clambering out of penal
shadow into an age dominated by the titanic struggle between
liberty and order, between freedom and authority, in the wake of
the French Revolution and the Napoleonic wars. The revolution
had proclaimed the Rights of Man. Simultaneously, it had re-
viled the Church, killed or imprisoned its leaders and disparaged
its faith. With the revolution crushed, if not the idea of revolution, and the monarchs restored to their insecure thrones, it
seemed inevitable that the Church would rally to the support of
order and authority, seeking to head off the anarchy which
travelled in the baggage train of revolutionaries demanding their
rights. Most Catholics on the continent accepted that it had to be
so, that the Church had no choice but to join forces with those
who would resist the anarchists. Some were troubled, however,
especially in France where wise men of Catholic faith could
perceive through the awful carnage and gunsmoke the prophetic
truth in the assertion of liberty. Wrote Alexis de Tocqueville:
'What has always most struck me in my country, and especially of
late years, has has been to see ranged on one side the men who
value morality, religion and order, and on the other side those
who love liberty and legal equality. To me this is as extraordinary
as it is deplorable; for I am convinced that all the things we thus
separate are indissolubly united in the sight of God. They are all
'sacred', if I may use the expression; men may be great and happy
only when they are combined'. The Irish of his day showed how
they could in fact be combined.

To unsympathetic observers — viz. British politicans and establishment figures — the popular democracy moulded by
Daniel O'Connell in Ireland was no more than a mob upon a
leash, a demagogue's weapon to threaten a government which
resisted his demands. To understanding observers — viz.

64

Tocqueville's friends Beaumont, Montalembert and others who came to see the phenomenon at first hand — what was happening in Ireland asserted the novel and exciting belief that the people's wishes might be made to prevail without resort to violence, subversion or disobedience of lawful authority lawfully exercised. It was sufficient to act politically: to pay the Catholic Rent, to attend Monster Meetings, to elect the right members to parliament. Where the English saw only unqualified 'agitation', the French (who knew what horrors constituted the reality of civil disturbance) saw an orderly marshalling of forces in pursuit of legitimate demands, and they marvelled that it could be done. Beaumont, expressing their bewilderment, described how they looked upon 'a nation constitutionally in revolt, agitated but not rebellious'. Thus was the first, pragmatic, fear eliminated. The demand for freedom did not have to be urged through anarchy. 'If they prevent us from talking politics', proclaimed O'Connell, 'why, we shall whistle or sing them'. The Irish would keep within the letter of the law, 'that shall be the extent of our obedience'. And again, 'I want you to get arms. Now mind me, do you know the arms I want you to get? The Repeal Society's cards! Everyone who has that is well armed'. *Aux armes, citoyens!* What a transmutation of meaning between Ireland and France ... the same phraseology, the same liberal objective of self-determination, but a methodology utterly different. The English caught the whiff of revolution; the French noted the constitutionality, the acceptance of a legal limitation to action, the substitution of political for military force, and they rejoiced at the discovery.

Political action was not itself the message which these liberal Catholics wanted to urge upon the Church of their time. What the political emphasis of the Irish movement gave them was the liberty to preach liberty, for it removed the automatic connotation of violence from the concept of the Rights of Man. Elements of their preaching were drawn from that Ireland as well, or at least reinforced by the virile advocacy of the Irish case. Two principles in particular would find their way into the teaching of the Second Vatican Council. The people whose political will O'Connell sought to make prevail were for the most part Roman Catholics. In his campaigns for emancipation, for better educational facilities, for the abolition of tithes, not only were the people for whom he sought relief Roman Catholics but the burdens they bore had originally been loaded upon them because of their religion. Yet never did O'Connell urge relief on the ground that it was the right of Catholics to be granted it. He never made *the religion of the majority* the reason why his coun trymen should be fairly treated. He argued instead for the right of persons not to be coerced. 'The right of every man to freedom of conscience' he declared to be 'equally the right of a Protestant in Italy or Spain as of a Catholic in Ireland'. When offered support in parliament if he would in turn vote for measures favourable to pro-slavery interests, he responded by praying 'may my tongue cleave to my mouth if for Ireland, even for Ireland, I forget the poor negro one hour!' His championing of Jews, Poles, Latin Americans belonged to the same context. The fact that later generations forgot the universality of O'Connell's vision, and forced his memory into a sectarian mould, diminish ed not a whit the immense contribution to the mind of the Church inherent in his insistence that rights pertain to *persons*, not to credal systems or to statistical proportions or to rulers tyrannic ally asserting their claims of legitimacy.

The second principle which the Church in time would make its own was related to the first. The idea of rights attaching to persons had roots in the secular philosophies of the eighteenth century. It received eloquent phrasing and practical application in the constitution of the newly-independent United States. It received a somewhat different and more dangerous phrasing in the *Rights of Man* promulgated by the revolutionary French. The point I make here is that the idea of personal rights as adopted by O'Connell, and carried into the mainstream of liberal Catholic apologetics, had its origin outside the Roman Catholic Church. It was a phenomenon of the then contemporary world. So far from disdaining it on that account, O'Connell and the liberal Catholics found it good, a recognition of human dignity which conformed to the Gospel and deserved to be blessed by the Church. The Irish Church raised no objection at the time to this endorsement of a world-generated concept, and no priest or bishop reprimanded O'Connell for identifying as 'religious duty' the attempt 'to terminate a system of fraud, perjury and oppres sion of the poor'. The great Dominican preacher and liberal Catholic, Henri-Dominique Lacordaire, would point dramatic ally to this confluence of religious and temporal understanding in his panegyric on the death of O'Connell: 'In denying the rights of man, we deny the rights of God ... the rights of God and human rights form a unity ... tyranny would be invincible if it were to succeed in destroying the idea of rights ... liberty is a work of virtue, a holy work and therefore a work of the Spirit'. The Irish insight, adopted and adapted by the French, thus acknowledged that the Spirit moves in the world as well as in the Church. It was a further optimistic note to add to the recognition that rights pertain to persons, and that to demand these rights need not be disruptive of order in society. The Church was thereby armed to make the cause of liberty its own.

The Church did no such thing. The days of O'Connell and Lacordaire were the days also of Gregory XVI and *Mirari Vos*. The oft-told story need not be repeated here. Enough to recall that Rome openly frowned upon individual freedoms: freedom of worship, freedom of the press, demands for civil liberty addressed to authoritarian monarchs. The Irish, seeking practical benefits for a people Catholic in the main and resorting to no violence, escaped notice. This was not what Rome had in mind, or so it seemed to a Rome scarcely more understanding of Ireland than were English politicians in London. Rome was speaking of the anti-clericals and the incipient state supremacists. But the liberal Catholics on the continent had to walk with care. To Rome they appeared to be theologising, and theologising away the sins of revolution at that. Perhaps it was good for them to be hard-pressed. It encouraged them to ponder, to hone and shape their thinking so that the freedom conforming to the Gospel stood in sharp contrast to the rational free-thinking more commonly in circulation. The Roman Question had reached crisis point, and Pio Nono was fixed in his views when the elderly Montalembert made a last effort in 1863 to voice the liberal perception. Unbridled freedom was far from what he sought: 'the fervent and practical cult of God made man is the indispensable counterweight of that perpetual tendency of democracy to establish the cult of man believing himself to be God'. That was to say, once man saw his rights were God-given and not man-invented, balance was attained, the anti-clericals were disowned and the Church could fairly be invited to pronounce a blessing. It was to be his last major assertion that liberty did not contradict religious faith. With it he coupled a last plea to look for the good in a secular idea. Might there not, he mused, be something to be said for the theory of a free Church in a free State? Rome sent him his answer: first, a private rebuke; then the cannonade of *Quanta Cura* and the *Syllabus of Errors*. The gate was clanked shut upon the Catholic liberals as firmly as the Porta Pia upon the advancing army of Italy.

That Rome had its reasons, none can deny, nor need they be elaborated here. The anti-religious, anti-Catholic, anti-clerical clamour in the air made it, humanly speaking, an inappropriate time to disentangle the acceptable from the unacceptable in the liberal ethos. What matters in hindsight is the extraordinary fact that for nearly a hundred years the *non possumus* of Pius IX stood unrevoked: 'If anyone thinks the Roman Pontiff can and should reconcile himself and come to terms with progreee, with liberalism and with modern civilisation, let him be anathema'. Unrevoked, but not, let it be said, unqualified. Some of the human rights preached with greater or less effect in the world attracted Church approval and support. Leo XIII initiated an era of papal concern for the rights of the worker. Benedict XV sought to assuage the horrors of war. Pius XI, despite his treaty with Mussolini, probably came close to appreciating the universal truth of human rights in his dawning awareness of fascist evil, but he died before he could bring the strands together. Pius XII, with the agony of war-time choices behind him, showed an incisive understanding of social phenomena like the press and the cinema. The Church leadership most certainly did not stand still in those years, nor was it oblivious to people's wants. What has to be said, from the easy vantage-point of post-conciliar awareness, is that the unhappy dualism — some would say manichaeism — of the mid-nineteenth century remained intact throughout the first half of the twentieth. In the eyes of many Catholics, a righteous Church faced an unrighteous world, and no Church authority contradicted the belief. If it was not altogether God against mammon, the spirit against the flesh, it was at any rate a Church possessed of the fulness of truth contrasted with a world reeking of error. And error had no rights. Protestants and unbelievers were entitled to toleration, but *not* to unfettered freedom in the public celebration of the faith that was in them, still less to freedom from civil laws anchored in Catholic doctrine. Such stern norms, of course, could be invoked only where Catholics predominated. Elsewhere, the Catholic Church, the perfect society, could demand for itself both full freedom of worship, and freedom from all oppression.

We should be slow to mock. The standards, to be sure, were illiberal but it was not a very liberal age. Empires were still about. Dictators and juntas ruled. There was Stalinism. There were democracies — France, Belgium, pre-fascist Italy and Spain — where the anticlericals often ruled overbearingly. Practical experience gave the Church no special reason to favour one political system above another. If it was gradually, very gradually, coming to perceive the virtues behind the mediocrity of democratic liberalism it was simply because — as Plato might have observed — that everything else was proving to be worse. It was also, and this would matter, because of the relative ease with which the Catholic Church found itself accomodated in the English speaking democracies: Great Britain, the white Commonwealth (then the *only* Commonwealth), the United States above all. Tocqueville, a hundred years earlier, had alerted those interested to the American experiment. Every priest he met there, he said, 'attributed the peaceful dominion of religion in the country to the separation of Church and State'. By the 1930s it was beginning to look as if this were the only context into which the Church could comfortably fit. By the end of the Second World War, Pope Pius XII was endorsing the virtues of democracy. The novelty of it, perhaps, was a little obscured by the Russian bear growling behind the Curtain. It sounded to the cynics as if the Church might simply be choosing its allies for a coming confrontation. The emergence of Church-favoured political parties calling themselves Christian Democrats confirmed the cynicism of some, proved the reality of conversion to others. The Church in fact was learning, albeit from a mixture of motives — seeing the good in democracy, seeing the advantage too. Right to the end of the 1950s, and in particular once the Christian Democrats became tainted with the ordinariness of ordinary politics, it could not be said with assurance that the Church had done more than endorse the democratic process for defensive purposes, much as it had endorsed Windhorst and his Zentrum in Bismarck's Germany or the Catholic politicians of early twentieth century Italy.

If it seems harsh to record a doubt regarding the Church — I mean the Church leadership in Rome and within the local Churches — in its Christian Democrat phase, remember that doubt makes a gentler judgment than denunciation. Franco's Spain still flourished, and Salazar's Portugal. Were they much criticised by the admirers of Adenauer and di Gasperi? Joe McCarthy came and went in America. Had the Church much to do with his going? We need not denounce, but we have to be slow to say that the dimensions of liberty had been comprehended and made its own by the Church of the 1950s. At best, there was groping, a consciousness that old ways would no longer serve in the post-war era, when so many could bear witness that Catholic and Protestant, Jew and atheist, liberal and conservative had all walked together the *via dolorosa* to Golgotha, the place of the skull.

But not everyone had known that harrowing ordeal. Few in

Ireland had known it and in Ireland the Catholic Church continued to display the curious mixture of characteristics to which its
adherents had become accustomed, an English puritanism cross-
bred with a Roman triumphalism. The prophetic Church of
O'Connell's time had died in the Famine. For reasons which
need not delay us here, its liberal vision had narrowed to mere
nationalist separatism, and its insistence that human dignity be
respected had changed to the assumption that Ireland was a
better, holier, more God-fearing and God-favoured country
than any other. Its people were to be protected from contamin-
ation by the materialist world beyond our shores. Church-
approved state censorship controlled the influx of books and
films. The imitation of secularist or 'worldly' standards was kept
at bay by legislation, ordinary and constitutional, informed by
Catholic teaching and sometimes expressed in the very language
of papal encyclicals. Contraception and divorce were thereby
inhibited. Catholic principles on the family, education and private property were buttressed by law. A Catholic ethos pervaded
society in independent Ireland.

Again, let us be slow to mock. There was great goodness in this
Irish Church, deep faith and much prayer. Its offspring provided
the mainstay of the Catholic population in America, Australia
and English speaking Canada. Its missionaries brought Christianity to many thousands in Africa and the Far East. Back at
home, it was the focal point of most people's life and culture, its
ostentatious self-righteousness notwithstanding. If it burdened
the Protestant minority with an irritating public reiteration of
Catholic attitudes, it did virtually no overt injury to Protestant
interests or Protestant conscience. As the late Jack White put it,
writing as an Irish Protestant about the aftermath of independence: 'It is not easy to think of another case in which a defeated
ascendancy has been treated with such exemplary generosity by a
victorious people. An Irish democracy converted a privileged
minority into an equal minority, not into an underprivileged or
subservient minority'.

At the same time, it has to be said that the Irish Church of the
day — and I mean not only the Church authorities but the
generality of people who constituted that Church — claimed and
exercised a right to assert itself which it recognised in no other
religious body. That Catholics and Protestants in their common
human dignity might enjoy exactly the same rights never occurred to it; never, anyway, in the sense that the Protestant might
have the right to do what the Catholic believed to be wrong. It

subscribed to a dualist *weltanschaung*, believing the world and its works to be perilous outside the safe haven of Catholic Ireland — the contrast to which was the country often described as 'pagan England'. It was not a Church, therefore, inclined to learn from the world or to ponder in a questioning spirit the premises on which rested its understanding of faith. This meant its theology was analytical rather than contemplative or innovative. It would find itself, as a result, at a grave disadvantage in conciliar discussion, where the bishops and *periti* from other local Churches had much new thinking to bring forward. The Irish Church leadership would also have a problem in promulgating the mind of the council to the Irish faithful, especially on matters where the council's position was literally foreign to what they had always believed. Among such matters liberty would loom large.

Liberty at the council arose for consideration primarily in discussing the Declaration on Religious Liberty although some of the most important issues involved were to be dealt with in the Constitution on the Church in the Modern World, technically and popularly known as *Gaudium et Spes*. Before either of these documents was anywhere near completion, however, the council was given an emphatic indication of the road to travel by John XXIII. Death awaited the wonderful old pope mere weeks away when he issued his encyclical *Pacem in Terris*. He knew his time was very limited, so we may legitimately see this celebration of man's dignity as Pope John's last testament, the words he chose to leave resounding in our ears and in the ears of the fathers of the council after he was laid to rest. Although *Pacem in Terris* acknowledges the rights to believe and to profess one's belief, to be informed, to work, to form associations and to participate in politics, and thus comes as close as makes no difference to rescinding the trenchant anathemas of Gregory XVI and Pius IX, its central teaching on the freedom rooted in human dignity avoids contradiction of what went before. Error continues to have no rights, but it becomes far more important to proclaim the entitlement of *persons* in error to all the 'rights of man'. The doctrine is simply stated: 'One must never confuse error and the person who errs ... The person who errs is always and above all a human being, and in every case he retains his dignity as a human person'. Since all human rights derive from human dignity, which in turn derives from God's intentions for mankind, any distinction between the possessors of truth and the mistaken has no relevance here. 'The rights of man', a phrase significantly used by the pope to mean what we usually now call human rights, can be demanded by everybody, not because everybody is right in what he or she believes, but because everybody is a human person endowed with human dignity. The pope goes further. He invites us to read, and respond to, 'the signs of the times'. In context, this means observing the world and distilling the good from it, gratefully learning the lessons it has to teach us. 'Constantly-evolving historical circumstances' can reveal acceptable features even in philosophies once condemned by the Church, and the hand of God can be seen in all who struggle for enlightenment, even if they remain entangled in 'the web of error'.

In *Pacem in Terris* Church and world are reconciled, and more than reconciled. Here is an end to manichaeism. Church and world remain distinct entities, but inseparable entities also. The Church addresses itself to the world. The world offers messages which the Church cannot ignore. The link is people, people of a common creation sharing a common destiny. People make up the Church. People make up the world. People are 'endowed with inteligence and free will .... redeemed by the blood of Jesus Christ .... the children and friends of God and heirs of eternal glory'. Within their multifarious activities will be found the signs of the times, and a Church which neglects to read these signs will stultify. The great mission of the Church is to reveal God to the world, not least by beaming the light of the Gospel upon the world's concerns. This mission can scarcely be discharged if the Church holds the world at arm's length. It long did so upon a plea for order, alleging that the freedom embodied in the rights of man put order in jeopardy. *Pacem in Terris* dismantles that dichotomy also. Order matters, matters hugely, but there can be no order without recognition of human dignity and the 'rights and duties' flowing therefrom. The duties come down to 'respecting the rights of others'. The question of order, therefore, leads back to rights, human rights which are 'universal, inviolable and inalienable'. Freedom being a pre-condition for order in human society and human dignity being the 'foundation' of order, true order cannot be attained to the exclusion of freedom. If it be doubted that the encyclical means precisely that, listen to what it says touching two themes related to order, namely the common good and authority: 'It is agreed that in our time the common good is chiefly guaranteed when personal rights and duties are maintained. The chief concern of civil authorities must therefore be to insure that these rights are acknowledged, respected, co- ordinated with other rights, defended and promoted, so that in in this way each one may more easily carry out his duties. For to safeguard the inviolable rights of the human person, and to facilitate the fulfilment of his duties, should be the essential office of every public authority'. The common good would be heard of again.

Two years later, after intense debate and in the light of many submissions, the Vatican Council adopted its Declaration on Religious Liberty. The council signalled at the outset that it intended to say say something new: 'the council intends to develop the teaching ... ' It also aligned itself firmly with *Pacem in Terris* by declaring that its subject related to 'the inviolable rights of the human person'. The declaration was in fact narrower in scope than the encyclical, since it confined itself to one of these rights only, the right to freedom in matters religious. On the meaning and implications of that right, it brought to bear the light engendered by Pope John. 'The right to religious freedom is based on the very dignity of the human person ... has its foundation not in the subjective attitude of the individual but in his very nature .... continues to exist even in those who do not live up to their obligation of seeking the truth'. It is hard to imagine the concept of rights-pertaining-to-persons being more emphatically underlined. Not only do those in error enjoy a human right to the full, but they continue to enjoy it if their error arises from their own culpability. And what was the right so thoroughly endorsed? 'Freedom of this kind means that all men should be immune from coercion ... so that, within due limits, nobody is forced to act against his convictions in religious matters in private or in public, alone or in association with others'. This was the first constituent of the right to religious freedom, there should be no coercion upon belief, no pressure on anybody 'to act contrary to his conscience'. The second constiuent was that nobody should be 'prevented from acting according to his conscience'. This copperfastened the teaching. People were not to be forced to do what their belief prohibited. Neither were they to be prevented from doing what their belief permitted. It was surely not chauvinism but a kind of folk-memory to catch the echo of a stentorian Irish voice, insisting on the equality between Catholic rights in Ireland and the rights of Protestants in Spain. There were other echoes too: John Henry Newman explaining conscience to the Duke of Norfolk, Madison warning in *The Federalist* against the undue influence of factions, the *Declaration of the Rights of Man* asserting the rights of others as the only legitimate restraint on the citizen's freedom. The Church was indeed making its own the

73

perceptions recorded within and outside its ranks alike. It was catching up.

There will be those to deny it, to allege that the Church comes by some process of internal combustion upon its doctrinal propositions. This overlooks the Church's role to illuminate the world's perceptions. It also contradicts the plainly evident influence of the world on the Church, which alarmed Pope John not at all. The most dramatic illustration I know of this influence occurs at the heart of the Declaration on Religious Liberty. Seeking a scriptural basis for the claim that mankind should be immune from coercion in matters of belief, the Council pointed to the example of the Lord himself and the apostles. Jesus Christ 'did not wish to be a political Messiah who would dominate by force... he bore witness to the truth but refused to use force to impose it... from the very beginnings of the Church the disciples of Christ strove to convert... not however with the use of techniques unworthy of the Gospel but above all by the power of the Word of God'. That example justified the Council in its claim that 'truth can impose itself on the mind of man only in virtue of its own truth, which wins over the mind with both gentleness and power'. Remarkably, the selfsame argument, appealing to the selfsame example, had been made nearly two hundred years earlier by Thomas Jefferson when he advocated a bill to provide for religious freedom in Virginia. Interference by force with man's freedom to form and hold his own opinions, said Jefferson, would be 'a departure from the plan of the Holy Author of our religion, who, being Lord of both mind and body, yet chose not to propogate it by coercions on either, as was in his almighty power to do, but to extend it by influence on reason alone'. So similar was the reasoning and the form of words in the two documents, it would be asking too much of coincidence to suppose that the writer of the council's statement had no knowledge of the American precedent. It was natural to surmise that Father John Courtney Murray, American Jesuit and political scientist, who drafted much of the conciliar document, had been behind the use of the American argumentation. Many years after the council, Cardinal Wright of the Roman Curia, himself an American, assured me this was not so. The Jeffersonian reference, he said, was brought forward at an early stage in the drafting by Cardinal Montini, Archbishop of Milan. In 1965, Cardinal Montini, by now Pope Paul VI, would promulgate the Declaration on Religious Liberty as the teaching of the universal Church.

In all of this I am anxious simply to make the point that neither the council nor its popes were averse to the world, to drawing upon its wisdom, to offering it the inestimable riches of the truth in the Church's keeping. If Pope John was not loath to speak about 'the rights of man', the core concept of the French Revolution, and Pope Paul could accept the guidance of the Protestant – perhaps deist – Jefferson, if a council of the Church could declare the rights of persons in error to be God–given, why are we so cautious in situations where the Church's understanding of human rights, the right of religious liberty in particular, could and should be invoked? By 'we' I mean the whole Church. I also mean the Irish Church.

The Declaration says that 'protection of the right to religious freedom is the common responsibility of individual citizens, social groups, civil authorities, the Church...' So what is the Church doing about it? I find it strange that there has been no pastoral instruction on implementing the declaration, no apostolic letter setting out the norms to be observed. I have never heard a sermon on religious liberty. Until the very time of writing these lines I have never seen the Church authorities refer to the declaration, of their own initiative, as an assemblage of principles binding the Church itself. The exception, a most welcome exception, occurs in the submission by the bishops of England and Wales in preparation for the 1985 Extraordinary Synod in Rome, where the declaration is noted to sustain the case for a recognition of a pluralism in the Church. It is difficult, of course, to prove a negative and I shall be only too happy if my comments here should elicit a correction, indicating other examples of ecclesiastical concern to see the teaching implemented.

There are, as it happens, two ways in which we may hear the conciliar doctrine urged but neither can really be said to propagate the central message. The first is when the Church claims the right of religious freedom for itself in circumstances where pressure is exerted on Catholics by civil authorities. True, the declaration stresses the right of Church members to enjoy religious freedom, and it would be ludicrous to suggest that a right proclaimed for all should not be available to Catholics. The demand is legitimate, but such cases cannot be used to represent the Church's commitment to protect the right, as the Council required it to do. To urge the right of Catholics to religious freedom goes no further *prima facie* than repeating once more the long-established attitude that the Church should be spared oppression. The question essentially posed for the Church by the declaration is whether it will defend the entitlement to religious freedom of persons who happen not to be Catholics. It should be remembered that the declaration was first conceived as a chapter for the council's Decree on Ecumenism. Add the emphasis on the rights of persons-in-error carried through from *Pacem in Terris*. Note also the adoption of secular perceptions of religious freedom, together with marked signs of papal approval for Catholics criticised in the past by the Church authorities because they advocated ideas with a secular origin: on the day after the council approved the final text of the declaration Pope Paul concelebrated Mass with some twenty theologians who had all been in difficulties with the Holy Office, Fr Courtney Murray among them, and on the morning when he promulgated the declaration he incorporated at the heart of the papal homily the thoughts, and very nearly the words, of Montalembert on the distinction between true and false freedom. There can really be no doubting the intent of pope or council that the Church should acknowledge and demonstrate its duty to care for the rights of others and concur belatedly with those who said as much in the past.

The second way in which the letter of the declaration can be quoted without necessarily touching on its spirit can be seen when Church authorities resist demands from the laity, or indeed from persons outside the Church, that the requirements of religious freedom be implemented in a specific situation. This normally happens when the State proposes to introduce legal change which will facilitate people in conduct disapproved by Catholic moral teaching — using contraceptives, for example, or remarrying after obtaining a divorce. If civil law prohibits such conduct in modern society, there is a manifest likelihood that it will infringe that immunity from coercion to which all people are entitled, an' immunity summarised in the declaration as 'freedom from interference in leading their lives according to their conscience'. To resist the appeal to religious freedom in these circumstances, the Church authorities will sometimes fall back on the qualificatory phrase 'within due limits', used by the declaration to indicate that the right to act upon belief cannot be treated as absolute. We are told, for example, that the introduction of divorce will lead to the collapse of moral standards, the destruction of the family, the opening of floodgates and other apocalyptic developments. The legal change proposed is therefore judged to exceed the due limit within which religious freedom applies. A glib but valid comment might be to wonder how it is that *every* appeal to religious freedom, in matters which bear upon Church teaching, run into this objection. It might fairly be asked why the council felt it proper at all to instruct the Church to have a care for the right of religious freedom since the Church apparently poses no obstacles which are not fully justified or justifiable. It might also be asked whether it is sufficient to *say* that certain consequences will follow and expect the exercise of an otherwise irrefutable right to be forbidden as a result. Jefferson had a formula that 'to restrain the profession or propagation of principles on supposition of their ill tendency is a dangerous fallacy, which at once destroys all religious freedom ... ' A fair point, for otherwise *my* unreasonable fear could be enough to destroy *your* undoubted right.

That there must be limits need not be argued. Jefferson conceded that civil government could rightfully 'interfere when principles break out in overt acts against peace and good order'. The important theme to grasp, in the declaration as in civil jurisprudence, is the bias in favour of the right to religious freedom. Says the declaration, 'the exercise of this right cannot be interfered with as long as the just requirements of public order are observed'. It is surely crystal clear that as long as 'the requirements of public order' have not *in fact* been abandoned, the exercise of the right *must not* be inhibited. It is simply not sufficient to *assert* that public order *will* break down. A forecast cannot undermine a right. Or to put the same argument in less extreme terms, the burden of proving that evil consequences will inevitably follow from the exercise of a right falls on those who so allege. It will indeed often be difficult to prove, for as many arguments will be raised against the allegation of evil consequences as in its support. So be it. Few will challenge the importance of protecting the young, safeguarding public morals and other considerations which trouble the critics of change. That the right to religious freedom takes precedence over all but facts proven beyond dispute, shows very well the pinnacle upon which the council lodged the developed doctrine. Acknowledging the rights of others, the council effectively stated, is as much a moral issue as anything connected with personal relationships or marriage. And while conceding that society must guard 'against possible abuses committed in the name of religious freedom', it insisted in this context as well that 'man's freedom should be given the fullest possible recognition and should not be curtailed except when and in so far as is necessary'. The priorities are evident.

The foregoing will be read as a reflection on the Irish Church.

So it is, and little more need be said about the misanthropic pessimism with which some Irish churchmen and laity look upon the world to which we belong and which belongs to all of us. Let us leave them to their profoundly unhistoric dualism and to the misery of their suspicions. Let us at the same time beware of the way in which they recruit the rest of us unwittingly into support for their arguments. They speak of 'the majority' and even of '95%', attributing common beliefs to these preponderances within the population. It is true that many Irish Catholics fundamentally disagree with the opinions of these preconciliar extremists. It is more important to realise that numbers have no relevance to rights. The rights of persons in a minority are as real as the rights of persons found to be in a majority. If this were not so, there would be little need for declarations of freedom, civil or secular, since the persons whose freedom stands most in peril are the members of national, cultural, political or religious minorities. Minorities, not least in Ireland, are at the mercy of the majorities among whom they live. It is their rights, therefore, that most need caring for by the Church, the government and the people. It is their rights which most need to be guaranteed, and it is consequently no surprise to discover the Declaration on Religious Liberty laying down that 'religious freedom must be given such recognition in the constitutional order of society as will make it a civil right', and again that religious freedom 'must be sanctioned by constitutional law'. Constitutional law is the instrument which can best protect minority rights. It is good to note that in Ireland over the past twenty years the High Court and Supreme Court have done a lot, through their interpretations of a seemingly flawed Constitution, to make the fundamental law into a bulwark for the protection of individual rights: among them the right to marital privacy, the right not to be impeded in exercising a right, the right not to be distinguished from others on the ground of religion, except as a protection against discrimination.

Irish politicians have tried too, with proposals, actual or tentative, to amend invidious laws on contraception, on illegitimacy, on the constitutional issue of divorce. Here, the pressure from groups who fail to allow for the difference between the right of the Church to preach its own doctrine and duty of the State to protect the rights of all its citizens (which is also Church doctrine!) has brought a slowing of effort. It has also made very difficult the serious discussion of serious questions which need to be examined with care. There has been much about floodgates,

78

of course, and that always decelerates popular approval for change in Ireland. Could the Church authorities give a better lead? Yes, by preaching the doctrine. But it would be wrong to imply that they have been inactive. The late Cardinal Conway made it clear that he had no wish to prevent removal of the constitutional clause recognising the 'special position' of the Catholic Church. On contraception legislation. the bishops' conference stressed that law-making was for the elected representatives of the people, a point repeated with emphasis in the bishops' oral submission to the New Ireland Forum. When it was proposed to write a ban on abortion into the Constitution, the episcopal bench declared itself in favour of the measure, but insisted that Catholics might in conscience take an opposite view and should not on that score be accused of advocating the introduction of abortion. The good record of the Irish Church in promoting assistance for the poor of the Third World might also be mentioned. It does not bear directly on religious freedom, but its advocacy for the rights of the down-trodden applies the message of *Pacem in terris* where it most needs to be heard. This is concern for the rights of others — as was even more precisely the bishops' promise to the Forum that they would raise their voices 'to resist any constitutional proposals which might infringe or endanger the civil and religious rights and liberty cherished by Northern Ireland Protestants'. In all this there is hope. That there are other voices within the Irish Church, voices with influence, has already been indicated. I think it legitimate to pray that the conciliar voices may prevail and that those who can bring this about may be granted the courage to do what has to be done, even if it means bishop openly differing with bishop.

Perhaps the saddest aspect of the post-conciliar Church's approach to religious freedom has been the apparent assumption that nothing more needs to be said. The belief in Rome at the height of the debate was quite the opposite. The declaration was then thought to require a more detailed theological elaboration than the council had time to provide for it. Religious freedom itself was seen to be no more than a huge theological field in need of ploughing. Fr Courtney Murray saw it as the opening chapter in the theology of freedom waiting to be written; had he lived he might have re-phrased the theme as a theology of human rights. Be that as it may, the theology has not emerged. The Irish, let it be said, tried to give a stimulus to the idea, and the international consultation on human rights, sponsored by the Irish School of Ecumenics in 1978, pointed to the kind of work which should be going on far more widely. It also illustrated the good which might have been achieved for the ecumenical movement. Liberty and human rights were virtually a *tabula rasa* for theologians. They were not, after *Pacem in Terris*, a matter of controversy between the Churches. Here, therefore, was a splendid opportunity for a joint enterprise, an ecumenical project in which theologians of many Christian traditions could work together in the hope of evolving a new insight acceptable to all because all would have contributed to its evolution. The Irish initiative did not draw the on-going response it deserved. It is probably now too late to begin, for, although there is no theology of freedom, there is a liberation theology. Liberation theology has its roots in the specific circumstances of the Church in a particular part of the world. It may also, as it develops, be seen to have a universal application. It sounds not unlike what happened in Ireland one hundred and forty years ago. What does that imply?

I am not competent to examine the controversial questions surrounding the Latin American vision or the Vatican's doubts regarding it. But it smacks of the future. That is enough. However it changes, however it accomodates itself to the rest of the Church and the more familiar aspects of the Church's teaching, it is posited on destitute, illiterate and oppressed masses in the underdeveloped continents. It must, it will, increasingly command the centre of the stage. What we have been calling liberty, the Rights of Man, spoke to the future in the same way in the wake of the French Revolution. O'Connell and the liberal Catholics were then prophetic. Their future has come and gone. We have lived through its latter days. In *Pacem in Terris* and the Declaration on Religious Liberty we see the Church coming to terms with a dying epoch. It could have come to terms more deeply and more broadly: that would have been the objective of the theology which might have been put in hand and which would have brought the Church fully up to date. Now the new future beckons, its theology already accruing. Of the champions of liberty long ago, among whom the Irish were first to be counted, we can say they stand proudly vindicated and we can but look with amazement on the quarrels now settled which some would keep alive among us in Ireland still. It was in 1848, I repeat in 1848, that Lacordaire preached on the witness of Daniel O'Connell and said: 'Catholics, listen to me closely. If you want freedom for yourselves, you must want it for all men and under every sky. If you seek it only for yourselves, it will never be granted to you. Bestow it where you are masters so that it may be given to you where you are slaves'.

The lesson for the universal Church is that it lives in history. Whenever it forgets, whenever it fails to hear a prophetic call from within the People of God, it drifts another degree away from the world to which it would bring the message of salvation. The story of religious liberty is, in large part, the story of a Church which opted out of time. The Second Vatican Council brought it back on course just as the new age was dawning. Liberation theology may well be the first challenge of that age to the values of the modern Church. The search for the God-given begins afresh. Let us open our ears to prophecy.

ENDA McDONAGH

A Church for the World

The Pastoral Constitution on the Church in the Modern World typifies in many ways the purpose and character of Vatican II. This council was not occasioned by any great doctrinal crisis, unlike its predecessors from Nicea to Trent. It did not propose any doctrinal decisions or definitions, unlike Vatican I. *Aggiornamento*, clearly expressing what John XXIII had in mind, and catchword of the sixties, had a pastoral ring. The 'up-dating' was to enable the Church to preach the Gospel more effectively in the modern world. The pastoral constitution, which was first mooted by Cardinal Suenens in the course of the council's work and not envisaged in the original schemata, sought to capture the essentially pastoral spirit of the council and the world-wide scope of its concerns. The *signs of the times* and the *agenda set by the modern world*, as the phrases went, were to be scrutinised by the council fathers in discerning the contemporary call of the Spirit and the contemporary significance of the Gospel.

The radical change in Church attitudes to the 'world' signalled by Vatican II may be illustrated most dramatically by contrasting the constitution of 1965 with the *Syllabus of Errors* of 1864. There are qualifications to be made, of course. The circumstances of a Church under siege from so many directions in the 1860s did not apply in the 1960s. (Yet if some of the council's preparatory documents and their sponsors — John XXIII's 'prophets of doom' — were to be taken at their face value, the siege mentality of a fortress Church (*Il Baluardo* of Cardinal Ottaviani) was still alive in Roman circles.) The adjustments to the modern world, and the increasing positive evaluation of its development, had begun in the Vatican with Leo XIII, succesor to Pius IX. Despite the crisis of Modernism in the 1900s and its small-scale replay in the 'fifties, that positive evaluation of the modern world by the Churches continued to grow even in Rome, particularly in social teaching and human rights (Leo XIII, Pius XI and Pius XII), in concern for peace (Benedict XV), in biblical studies and in understanding of the role of science (Pius XII). In

82

the world Church, as it now really was, from Asia and Africa to the Americas, new life and vigour and distinctive experience were preparing the way for a challenge to European traditions and norms. But reading the positive signs in that ambiguous century from Syllabus to Vatican II could scarcely have prepared many council fathers for the radicality and richness of what came to be known, by its first words, as the constitution *Gaudium et Spes*, 'Joy and Hope'. The very words themselves seemed an unlikely slogan to people used to the ascetic, almost grim, features of Pius XII or to the standard newspaper headlines, 'Church condemns', and 'Bishops warn'.

The change of mood was no mere ecclesiastical reflection of the 'swinging sixties', although the Church undoubtedly influenced and was influenced by the cultural, political and economic optimism of the times. For a short time, the two Johns, Pope and United States President, seemed together to symbolise that 'new frontier', new humanity in which a real liberation of humankind from fear and oppression, hunger and war, was possible. For the council fathers, mood was less significant than the slow, critical acceptance of the intellectual, political and scientific achievements of the previous two hundred years, from which the Church at the highest level had been generally insulated and to which it was frequently reistant. The values of the Enlightenment, of the liberal revolution, combined with the associated development in the physical and human sciences were now largely accepted and critically integrated into much of the Church's life and thinking. *The Church in the Modern World* was the highlight of this development, but many other Vatican II documents, such as that on Religious Liberty, on Revelation (with the subsequent statement on the study of the Gospels), on Ecumenism and non-Christian religions, even on the Church itself, reflected much of the modern view of humanity, which had sprung from the European Enlightenment.

Gaudium et Spes, although stemming from a council which represented a world Church in a sense hitherto impossible, remained basically a European document. The strong North American influence was European in origins, tone and concern. The rest of the world Church largely echoed the European dominance which so many particular countries had shaken off politically — but not culturally, economically or religiously. The break-through achieved by the document remains of world significance because at least the particular crises tackled, political organisations and human rights, peace and war, economic power, marraige and the family are common to all. And the manner of speaking and thinking, for all its European provenance, has, for the historical reason of earlier European imperialism, relevance for very many of the cultures, countries and Churches of the rest of the world. But — and the *buts* come tumbling out — for Asians and Africans and Latin Americans, for those on the fringe of Europe like Ireland, for those on the other side of the great Europen divide in Poland and the other socialist countries, even for the peoples most directly concerned with the legacy of the Enlightenment in central and western Europe and North America, a balanced appreciation of such an adventurous and exciting document as *Gaudium et Spes* must also look at some of the limitations.

These will emerge, I hope, by attending the more specific purpose of this article — a consideration of the Church as the believing people of this island of Ireland, in the Irish circumstances of the mid-eighties rather than Europe of the mid-sixties. Ireland is now, politically, economically and culturally more fully and consciously part of Europe than it was in the 1960s. Accession to the European Economic Community has focussed much attention on Brussels and Strasbourg, in political and economic matters, while cultural and recreational links with other European centres have increased enormously. In other ways Ireland and Europe are more consciously integrated into the global village of the world. A reflection on the theme of 'Church in the World' will be more aware of the distinctiveness of (local) Churches and (local) worlds, while also sensitive to the intimate interlinking of these Churches and of these worlds.

1. A POSITIVE ADVENTURE: THE GIFT AND CHALLENGE OF MODERNITY

By seeking to integrate into a Christian perspective the positive values of two centuries of political and scientific progress, Vatican II offered a considerable challenge to believers everywhere. This was certainly true of Ireland. The relationship between Catholicism and democracy in Ireland in the early nineteenth century had been a matter of some admiration among European Catholics. And the transition in the early twentieth century from colony to stable parliamentary democracy might, in the light of the subsequent break-up of European empires, be no less worthy of admiration. In this respect no one could claim that the political legacy of the Englightenment had no impact in Ireland. Yet it remained true that the relationship between the Catholic commitment of the great majority of the Irish people and liberal political values was never properly worked out in theory or in practice. In the decades between independence and Vatican II, various circumstances at home (economic difficulties, for example) and abroad (the rise of communism and fascism) combined to obscure the basically liberal and social thrust of Irish deomcratic republicanism. In the changing circumstances of the 1960s Vatican II provided the spark for many thoughtful Irish Catholics and Protestants as they sought explicit reconciliation between their Christianity (Catholic and Protestant), their Irishness and their citizenship of the modern world. The advances and regressions which Irish Christians, as Churches and as individuals, have experienced over the last twenty years reflect their further struggles in search of dynamic reconciliation between their Christian, Irish and modern strands.

The suspicion of human reason, human freedom and human progress which characterised so much of the Catholic Church's attitude over two hundred years accorded poorly with an older tradition which had defended basic human goodness against innumerable dualist and manichaean movements and had resisted the very pessimistic view of humanity espoused by certain reformers. The earlier theologies which reached their climax in the work of St Thomas Aquinas, and the later ones which took their inspiration from him, should be very unhappy with the Syllabus of Errors and its associated attitudes. *Gaudium et Spes* with other documents of Vatican II finally overcame that suspicious mentality. Catholics need no longer feel guilty about being members of intellectual, cultural and political movements shaped by Enlightenment values. They could be truly 'modern', even if, like everybody else who took the Enlightenment seriously, they should not be uncritical acceptors of what passed for modernity.

Documentary regard for reason, personal freedom and social progress is no guarantee of adequate practice, in Church or State. Too many State constitutions and political programmes which enthusiastically endorse these values have little effect in practice. The Proclamation of 1916, the Democratic Programme of the First Dáil, and a series of subsequent documents including the 1937 Constitution, have proclaimed ideals and ambitions for the Irish people which have only been partially realised and sometimes openly abandoned. Church leaders and members are not necessarily better than politicians and citizens in implementing their own finest aspirations. Yet the openness which has characterised the Catholic Church over the past twenty years, for all the confusion and tensions to which it has frequently led, is a splendid achievement. Such openness has influenced the Church in Ireland, as the pages of *Doctrine and Life*, under the editorship of Austin Flannery, bear witness. The reasonable and fairminded examination of controversial topics, the respect for the personal freedom and integrity of those who differ, the recognition that social privation and oppression are of human making and require human re-making: there has been improvement in all these areas, essential as they are to the health of Irish society and to the health of the Churches in Ireland. The struggle to establish them received considerable impetus with Vatican II and the *Church in the Modern World.*

The shadows of the eighties, after the bright lights of the sixties and seventies, have underlined the fragile nature of respect for reason, freedom and social progress in many countries, including Ireland. The Churches must recognise their responsibility in protecting these essential human values in their own internal structures and conversations, and in their contribution to the wider society. It is not an unusual irony of history which finds Church leaders protecting human rights and values of which their predecessors were suspicious. The irony is multiple. Some of the greatest threats to enlightenment values have come from people who consciously espoused that tradition. Churches, which resisted the tradition and now promote many of its values, were often in their past resistant to these values, betraying some of the deepest and best strands in their own traditions. The recovery of the humanism of Thomas Aquinas, or the acceptance of humanity 'joy and hope, grief and anguish' (paragraph 1) by *Gaudium et Spes* does not preclude further ironic twists in their attitudes and practices. The Churches, Irish and universal, have in the recent past occasionally surrendered to fear and restrictiveness out of keeping with the grand vision of Vatican II.

The challenge of modernity accepted by *Gaudium et Spes* called for a Christian believer of conviction, integration, and commitment. Conviction, far from being blind and unreasoning, develops through an honest wrestling with the real and reasonable difficulties presented by life in the world today. Difficulties which penetrate mind and heart and bones and finally disintegrate bodily life are not banished by repeating the formulae learned in childhood. Adult faith is the fruit of adult struggles. Such adult faith can be craggy and awkward for oneself and one's guides. The administrative comfort of an unquestioning Church in a world of questions can only undermine genuine Christian faith. It is the responsibility of Church leaders and ministers, whether ordained or not, to provide a context in which people's real questions may be honestly voiced and fairly explored. That mandate from Vatican II, now more urgent in Ireland, is as yet far from adequate fulfilment. Adult theology groups, developments in catechetics, more critical and intelligent religious publications, occasional radio and television programmes, all contribute to the development of faith by personal conviction among a wide range of Irish people. The search for superficial 'supernatural' phenomena does not. The task is enormous, and some of the labourers do not seem entirely convinced.

Integration, as a feature of the Christian believer, enables one to cherish every aspect of the world as God-given in creation and God-accepted in incarnation, redemption, and resurrection. Flight from this world of God involves flight from God. The celebration of the cosmos, of the gifts of creation, is central to *Gaudium et Spes*, in terms which echo de Chardin's vision of the cosmos as the divine *milieu*. And with the gifts of creation come the gifts of creativity, which God has shared with humanity, and which issue in both the humble and the masterly achievements of human culture. From the simple sentence to Dante's *Divine Comedy*, from cave scratching to Picasso's *Guernica*, from basic drum-beat to final symphony, from stone-sharpening to laser beam, the astonishing creativity of human beings has extended the beauty and power of the cosmos, has created a new world of culture and technology. The *gaudium* is multiplied as Paul Henry's Achill joins the Achill we know. The *spes* is indefinitely expanded as technical expertise heals disease and overcomes drought and desert. There is a lot of celebrating to be done, a lot of thanksgiving, of standing in awe before the Himalayas and the Parthenon, of attending to the achievement of, the mastery of, so many things in nature and in culture.

A more ancient Irish Christianity rejoiced in natural beauty and erupted in cultural achievement. The civilization, in Kenneth Clark's terms, which the Irish monks preserved, developed and restored to Europe, was often cultivated in places of wild natural beauty like the islands of Sceilig and of Aran. The monks felt the pulse of that beauty in their own spiritual pilgrimages while in learning, language and illustration they carried on the sacred heritage of human cultural creativity.

Nineteenth century restoration of Irish Catholicism had not the time or resources or sensibility to renew that tradition. The impoverishment was reinforced by general Church suspicion of the current trumpeting of human achievement. In regard to one of the greatest created and creative gifts, sexuality, a dualism, which was not peculiarly Catholic or Irish, exercised a very diminishing influence. The treatment of sex and marriage in *Gaudium et Spes* resumed the celebratory attitude which the Hebrew and Christian traditions had, at their best, enjoyed. The impact of this development was very noticeable in Ireland. With better preparation for couples, and a greater sense of love and life, sex and marriage could be more fully integrated as gifts of God and more deeply celebrated as human joys.

The hope, like the joy, was also in and of this world and not just displaced to the next. It connected with human and social progress, which had been such a feature of western civilization in recent centuries. Human goodness and human ingenuity should and could harness the resources of the cosmos to overcome poverty, oppression and disease. Like Peadar O'Donnell's Islanders, most people in the world die when they die because they are poor. The council voiced its hope of overcoming this poverty unto death, so that all might live in accordance with their God-given human dignity. Despite its essentially hopeful message, the council did not ignore the fact of persistent and widespread oppression and the deep-rooted obstacles to its removal. And it was well aware of the dangers to the lives of nations and peoples from war as well as from poverty and injustice. Discussion of the subject included a clear rejection of total warfare, and of those acts of war 'directed to the indiscriminate destruction of whole cities or vast areas with their inhabitants' (paragraph 80). The reappraisal of war in the light of nuclear weapons, for which the document calls, had already begun.

The hope of progress towards an international community maintaining peace between nations and ensuring respect for the rights of individuals, which the council shared with the aspirations of the United Nations Charter, made better sense in 1965, perhaps, than in 1985. Yet, both the constitution and the charter are critical markers for Christians and their fellow-humans in the continuing struggle for peace and justice. They provide markers for Irish people also, whose need for peace and justice at home, and whose commitment to it abroad, have greatly intensified since the council. It may be at this point that one should move from considering the remarkable positive achievements of the constitution and their persisting validity, to the limitations which derive partly from its origins, and partly from the changed circumstances of the world in which the Church now has to function.

2. MAKING ROOM FOR THE TRAGIC

The Western/Northern-European dominance of the Church up to and including Vatican II did, as indicated earlier, greatly influence the agenda, the approach and the style of *Gaudium et Spes*. The distinctiveness and limitations of that European mode were quickly exposed in Latin America, as the Churches there sought to relate achievements and aspirations of the Council, and particularly the teaching on Church and world, to their condition of poverty and oppression. 'Liberation theology' and 'Church of the Poor', already widely accepted by the time of Medellin in 1968, revealed a very different agenda and approach from the liberal concerns and attitudes of Rome in 1965. Actually, *Gaudium et Spes* itself, as well as papal documents on issues of justice and peace (*Mater et magistra, Pacem in Terris* and *Populorum Progressio*) prepared the way for this more radical analysis of the Church in the world, and for the more radical response needed. The temptation to individualism, which liberal reforms frequently involve, and from which *Gaudium et Spes* did not entirely escape, becomes irrelevant in the context of the mass poverty and privation faced by the Churches in Latin America and other third world areas. The economic form of liberalism in particular, with its powerful and powerless, centre and periphery, dominant and dominated in a so-called world market economy becomes an instrument of oppression of the powerless, the peripheral and the dominated. The west, the north, Europe — in their oppressive roles — no longer provide the Christian inspiration and theological analysis which southern/third world countries need. Theological imperialism also must come to an end. *Gaudium et Spes*, despite its great positive achievements, which have validity also among the deprived, must be supplemented and eventually transformed in these very different worlds.

Even for a European country like Ireland, but on the continent's periphery, for long politically colonised and still economically very dependent, *The Church in the Modern World* could not always read correctly the signs of the times. The Enlightenment values of respect for reason, for individual freedom and for social progress, were however at least as much in need of critical integration into Irish Catholic thought and life as anywhere in Europe. That integration is still incomplete if one is to judge by

89

some of the topics and the manner of current public controversy.

The most serious limitation in the constitution applies to central as much as to peripheral Europe, as much to the dominant countries of the west as to the dominated elsewhere. In reading the signs of the times, insufficient attention was paid to the tragic dimensions of the history of Europe in the twentieht century. The fall of empires, the experience of two great fratricidal wars, the east-west division after 1945, and, above all, the chilling counter-sacrament of the Holocaust, summarise a tragic transformation of Europe in the fifty years leading up to Vatican II. As so many council fathers and most theologians (mainly European) had actually lived through so much of that tragic experience, it is all the more surprising how little explicit and existential impact it had on their deliberations and conclusions.

It could be argued that the council as a whole, and the pastoral constitution in particular, wished to offer a message of hope to the world and not engage in a depressing review of recent tragedy. This might be more urgent in view of the frequently negative reactions of the Church of Siege in the nineteenth and early twentieth centuries to the achievements and aspirations of the secular world. And the constitution did intend to deal with the grief and anguish, as well as the joy and hope, of humanity. In the immediate aftermath the response in Church and in world confirmed the judgement of the bishops and theologians in adopting such a positive stance.

After twenty years, and still grateful for the achievement, it is important to reflect on the failure to deal more fully with the tragedy of humanity as it developed in twentieth century Europe. Theological and ecclesiastical discussion of tragedy and evil can sometimes be self-righteous in its attitude, trivialising in its analysis, and banal in its prescriptions. The recent tragedy of Europe was a tragedy of Christians, of the Church. Christian believers and leaderes were directly implicated in the fratricidal wars. The genocidal programme which issued in the Holocaust had deep and tangled anti-Semitic roots among Christians, and could only develop so successfully because too few had the insights and courage to resist.

Until European Christians are able to confront their failure and recognise the tragedy and evil of this century, their expressions of solidarity with the sufferings and hopes of the rest of humanity will remain rather superficial. Here lies the most serious theological flaw in *Gaudium et Spes*. Hope does not evade failure, tragedy, evil. In the Christian pilgrimage hope arises through and beyond failure. For St Paul, 'suffering produces endurance, endurance produces character, and character produces hope' (Rom 5:3-4). Endurance, confronting, and wrestling with the suffering, precede hope. Paul's hope is based on the death and resurrection of the Lord. Death, with its darkness and destruction, must be fully accepted by Jesus before his acceptance by the Father in resurrection. The cries of need and near-despair in Gethsemane and on Calvary expose the tragic depths of human destruction and human abandonment. The acknowledgement of all that is a necessary prelude to the gift of hope.

The tragedy of Europe could be the beginning of truly Christian hope. But first, Christians must accept their own failure, their own responsibility, their own contribution to the imperialism, self-righteousness and destructiveness which characterised so much recent European history. The Holocaust and anti-Semitism are particular signs of the times for Christians. Yet even the the admirable attempt, in the council's document on non-Christian religions, *Nostra Aetate*, to move away from the traditional Christian treatment of the Jews does not properly face the Holocaust or Christian involvement in it. To acknowledge the tragedy and our complicity in it, is essential to the hope embodied in Christian conversion.

Ireland has had its own share of fratricidal killing and of Christian involvement in the tragedy. The last sixteen years in particular have exposed the violence between brothers, both Irish and both Christian. So far, as a people and as Churches, we seem unable to acknowledge the destructiveness which is in us, and which is fuelled by some deadly combination of our political, racial and religious alliegances. The Irish Churches in the Irish world may not take into themselves the motto *Gaudium et Spes* until they first acknowledge their role in maintaining the *luctus et angor* 'the grief and anguish' of the people of our time (par. 1). That grief and that anguish extend in Ireland to a wide range of people, handicapped and deprived in a variety of ways. How hope of relief, liberation, fulfilment may be conveyed in Christ's name to the mentally and physically handicapped, to the chronically and terminally ill, to the homeless, to the Travellers, to the unemployed, to prisoners, to homosexuals, to all the other deprived minorities, to women in their more general frustrations and privations, is a daunting set of tasks. Without sharing the suffering, acknowledging complicity, and working for change, Christians have no right to speak of hope. This may be more deeply true of the 'national question' where Church affiliation has always been a contributory factor. When Irish Christians finally and fully acknowledge that, we may hope to hope.

3. DÓCHAS LINN?

For the world that is Ireland now, the Catholic Church has much to cherish and develop from the Constitution *Gaudium et Spes*. A Church which understands itself as at the service of the Kingdom of God, proclaimed and inaugurated by Jesus Christ, will be on the alert to discern and promote these kingdom values of truth and freedom, justice and peace. It is not easy for the Church as people or hierarchy to remember its servant status. There is a natural self-inflation of Church and Church-leaders which permits human persons and institutions to obscure and even replace the reign or kingship of God. A parallel, more frequent, and more far-reaching self-inflation by State and politician, forgetful in turn of *their* serving role, leads to Church-State confrontations and sacred-secular power struggles, absorbing energies which should be spent, at least for the Church, in loving service.

Resistance by the Church to activities of the State may well be required in fidelity to its mission. So, for that matter, may resistance by statesmen to certain activities of churchmen. Tension and conflict can never simply be wished away. Yet the Church's mission to transcend the power-structures and the power-struggles of the princes of this world by loving and liberating service on the model of Jesus should make Church-leaders sensitive to the temptations of power within the Church itself and in the wider society. This applies with particular force to the Irish Churches, Catholic and Protestant, south and north. In their internal treatment of their own members they convey to many people a sense of difficulty with the *different* that may easily become intolerance. James Good and David Armstrong may have received exceptional treatment but they are limit cases of a pressure which many others have experienced. In the broader society, the restrictive and repressive roles of the Churches appear more significant to many people, not all of them enemies. Without confusing liberty with trivialising permissiveness, the Churches might well concentrate their efforts, for a year at least, on translating and promoting, in Irish ecclesial and political terms, the great Pauline theme of 'the freedom of the Christian'. If the Churches, in their separateness and together, took a year out to explore, preach, and actively implement the multiple dimensions of freedom, human and Christian, they would render signal service to Gospel and culture, to Kingdom and society.

Ireland and the Irish Churches would have much to record in terms of both joy and hope.

Ireland as tragedy should provide a constant counter to the promethean tendencies of unexamined liberalism or progressivism. With our sense of history and experience of failure we should be able to supply the tragic dimension missing from *Gaudium et Spes*. A sense of tragedy may also be self-indulgent and self-inflating. It has been so too often in Ireland. Drowning in our sorrows, we have sometimes become exhibitionists and escapists who refuse to confront, or attempt to overcome, our own real self-made problems. Recognising the tragic side of life is not, in Christian faith, an excuse for evading life but an opportunity for enduring through suffering, hoping through endurance, and so entering into transformation. The fatalism of 'It will be all the same in a hundred years' may swing to a trivial consumerist 'Eat, drink and be merry', without any serious effort to combine the sense of life as adventurous call, with a sense of the tragic. Where *Gaudium*, genuine rejoicing in life, is maintained in creative interchange with the 'the notion of some infinitely gentle, infinitely suffering thing', the *Spes*, Christian *hope*, that goes through and beyond Calvary in resurrection, is an authentic possibility.

MAURA HYLAND

Epilogue: What People of God?

When Vatican II ended, I was a teenager, and mostly unaware of the momentous things that were happening in high Church circles. In senior primary school, I remember having to memorize the Latin Mass responses. If one were a boy, that was o.k. Even if you didn't understand them, at least you usually got to use them. If one were a girl, it was, at best, good practice in tongue twisting.

I remember the stirrings that ushered in the change to the vernacular at Mass, and the discussions that accompanied the priest's change of position to face the people. I heard the vague misgivings of my elders. I was also aware of the wave of jubilation that spoke of 'opening windows', 'letting in fresh air', and that promised great things for the future. I wasn't too sure what all the fuss was about, but I was quite happy to be carried along on the institutional tide.

So much for teenage reminiscence. Twenty years later, one has a different perspective: a hunch that the real task of today's Church is that of looking to the future while struggling to find a point of contact with people living in the last quarter of the twentieth century for whom it is difficult to find either meaning in the present or hope for the future. The time has gone for gazing into the past and rejoicing at what has been achieved. Over half the population of our country are under thirty. So, let us remember that Vatican II, for many the great watershed in the life of the Church, is history for those who will build the Church of tomorrow. With an awareness of the past, from which we have come, and a deep consciousness of all the inadequacies and possibilities of the present, it is now time to take determined, if tentative, steps towards the future.

We must also remember that, since Vatican II, there has been Medellin (1968) and Puebla (1979). It is discouraging when we realize that, while other parts of the world are struggling with the far more challenging demands of these (Medellin, Puebla), the Irish Church is still trying to wrestle with the demands of Vatican II.

There are many areas that deserve careful consideration. In Ireland religious practice is still high. Our Sunday morning churches are still relatively full, and so the recorded decline among young people has not caused any real sense of alarm.

However, it would be dangerous to allow ourselves to become complacent. A closer look at our packed Sunday morning churches would show a low level of participation. The European Values Systems Study[1] shows that only 28% of those who attend Mass receive Holy Communion each Sunday, and almost half of those who say it is wrong to miss Mass on Sunday have purely legalistic reasons. This would indicate that, in another context, many of those who attend Mass would in fact stay away altogether. One difficulty is found in the lack of identity of the modern parish as a community that shares a common life, a common vision, and can therefore find meaning in common worship. Another difficulty is the quality of the Sunday celebration. Some work has been done, considerable in places, on the quality of these celebrations. But often the question is avoided of how relevant the Sunday celebration is to the daily lives of the congregation, which often has an age range from four to eighty. With the best will in the world, because of numbers, participation has to be limited.

While some are still happy to assume the role of passive participant or, worse than that, of spectator at the Eucharist, many are not. It is on rare occasions, when the Eucharist is celebrated by smaller groups, that the People of God are given the opportunity to decide on a theme, to choose the readings, to make explicit their concerns in a shared homily or in shared prayers. It is then that we can see the limitations imposed by large numbers, the limited time available, the formal structures of the building, and the diverse needs and expectations of the congregation at our Sunday celebrations. There is, surely, place for such parish celebrations, but perhaps there is also a growing need to give people the opportunity to experience a Eucharistic celebration where concepts such as community, participation, ministry, can be made real.

Rampant clericalism still characterises the Irish Church. Two factors seem to be involved. Firstly, we have a laity who for years had been trained to do as they were told, without expecting to be consulted, and without any sense of responsibility for the decisions that were taken by others. They are, only slowly, being re-educated to take ownership of the Church, to recognise their potential, and to be aware of their duty to make their voice heard.

Secondly, we have a clergy who are trained to see themselves as authority figures, running one-man shows, and are slow to face the risk of dialogue, of sharing responsibility, or even of taking seriously the voice and the experience of the laity. In this situation, many lay people react with anger and frustration, and many of the clergy by becoming even more authoritarian and withdrawn.

In *Evangelii Nuntiandi*[2] (1975), Pope Paul VI, after pointing out the importance of the active presence of the laity in the fields of politics, society, economics, culture, the sciences, the mass media, wrote: 'One cannot, however, neglect or forget the other dimension: the laity can also find themselves called, or be called, to work with their pastors in the service of the ecclesial community, for its growth and life, by exercising a variety of minsitries according to the grace and charism which the Lord in pleased to give them ... It is certain that side by side with the ordained ministries, whereby certain people are appointed pastors and consecrate themselves in a special way to the service of the community, the Church recognises the place of non-ordained ministries which are able to offer a particular service to the Church'. And, six years later, writing in an Irish context in an article entitled 'Decline or New Life',[3] Bishop Cahal Daly said, with reference to the laity: 'It is to our embarrassment as pastors that we must confess that they are as yet a largely untapped resource. We must get to work to develop this underdeveloped potential'.

A few years have since passed, but it is, without doubt, still true that the potential of the laity is still waiting to be tapped. There are some signs of hope, and proof that things can be different. In situtations where a genuine effort has been made to recognise the diversity of gifts in the community, all can find dignity and purpose, and be enabled to find their identity and live out their true calling as People of God. It should not be difficult to bring this about. There is a growing awareness of the emerging needs of the Christian community, for instance, in the area of on-going education and formation. For too long, the Church has put all its educational resources, both personnel and financial, into the school system. There is a definite opening for the development of lay ministries such as parish catechist or lay pastoral worker. The need is obvious, and there are lay people waiting for the opportunity to become involved. It is time to take seriously what was identified as a priority of the Irish bishops at their meeting in Mulrany in 1974: 'The main thrust of the Irish Church over the next five years should be the implementation of the principle of the involvement of the laity in the spiritual mission of the Church'.

Then there is the question of young adults and their perception of themselves in relation to the Church. I have already referred to the fact that among this age group there is a noticeable decline in religious practice. But this is merely a symptom of a much more serious disillusionment with the Church on the part of young people. A generation keenly aware of issues such as justice, violence, unemployment, who live in a consumer society and have its values presented very attractively by the mass media, call on the Church to be a leaven in Irish society. A recent picture in *The Irish Times* of a nun being arrested for standing with Travellers in Tallaght spoke far more eloquently to the young people in our Church than do lengthy statements from Church leaders that often seem out of touch with reality and do not promise action in the future.

In the past, it was fairly certain that, when the message of the Gospel was preached at Mass on Sunday, the same values would be made explicit in the life of the home and of the community. This is no longer the case. Young people today challenge us to validate our message by living it out in our daily lives. They search for authenticity, and often this is not obvious in our Church. Young people are not interested in passive participation. They want a role, they want to play their part. 'Listen to what we are saying!' is their challenge to the Church. 'If you want us to see you as relevant, then, hear our voice, get to know our concerns, and then, perhaps, we can find a meeeting point'. A generation that finds little hope in a future threatened by nuclear war, beset by unemployment, violence and injustice, is ready to look to the Gospel of Jesus Christ for hope and for a direction forward. Have we got a Church that can preach that Gospel with conviction and give it the witness it demands?

In the Report presented by the Working Party established by the National Conference of Priests of Ireland it states as a recommendation: 'That priests ask themselves the following questions — a) Are women seen by the Church as people in their own right? b) Are women properly listened to, and responded to? c) Are women often only tolerated as an unpaid but willing workforce for the performance of menial tasks? d) Do Church structures contradict the dignity of women as proclaimed in Church

97

documents and in the Gospel message? e) Since women comprise 50% of the Church membership, should they not expect, then, to carry a proportionate degree of responsibility for management of Church affairs?'

The failure on the part of many of our clergy to address these questions and the other recommendations of the Working Party honestly is giving rise to widespread alienation from the Church among women. The Church will lose much richness is she loses the insights, perspectives and commitment of interested women. Some areas which need attention by the official Church at the moment are: The inadequate representation of women on Church commissions and on policy-making bodies; The unnecessary use of alienating sexist language in liturgies; The exclusion of women on occasions when large groups of priests concelebrate; The fact that Church teaching represents an exclusively male point of view especially in the area of sexual morality; The tendency to involve men more freely than women in parish work.

A failure on the part of the Church to listen to, dialogue with, and reflect on the articulated experience of women would be, not only for women, but for the Church itself, a real source of impoverishment.

At this time, then, the Church in Ireland needs to acquire a new awareness of the aspirations and needs of its people. Today's people are ready, perhaps more ready than ever before, to listen to a Church that speaks to and interprets their experience, that shows them how to work with these experiences in the light of the Gospel, and that enables them to walk with hope towards the future. The challenge for the Church is to begin to see itself no longer as a hierarchical institution but as a serving community — a challenge for laity and clergy alike, the same challenge that Jesus presented to his apostles the night before he died, when, having washed their feet, he said: 'Do you understand what I have done to you? You call me Master and Lord, and rightly; so I am. If I, then, the Lord and Master, have washed your feet, you should wash each other's feet. I give you an example so that you may copy what I have done to you'. (Jn 13:12-14)

And there are real seeds of hope; a new vitality, a questioning, even an excitement are part of what people are experiencing where initiatives have been taken. All is far from lost. But renewal on a much wider scale is needed, a renewal that embraces the concerns of all those who are the Church. This can happen only in a Church that is a pilgrim Church, that doesn't have to produce pat answers to all questions, that is prepared to search, that is itnerested in service rather than in power, that values the dignity of all its people, that takes risks, that challenges not only in word but in witness the values of the modern world, that stands with rather than alienates the poor, the oppressed, the voiceless, in short, a Church that takes seriously the Gospel of Jesus Christ.

Such a Church cannot have numbers as one of its primary concerns; this could probably be a smaller Church but with enthusiastic commitment as the defining characteristic of its people; it could, in fact, become, as Jesus Christ calls it, 'the light of the world'.

Notes

INTRODUCTION

1. Austin Flannery, O.P., (ed.) *Vatican Council II: Conciliar and Post-Conciliar Documents*, Dublin, Dominican Publications, 1975. Revised edition, Dublin, Dominican Publications, 1981.

TO BE ONE

1. *Acta Apostolicae Sedis*, Vol. 20, no. 1 (Jan. 1928), p. 14. This encyclical was the response to the Lambeth Conference of 1920, the encyclical of the Orthodox Ecumenical Patriarch (1920) and the organisers of the Life and Work Conference at Stockholm (1925) and Faith and Order Conference at Lausanne to participate in the ecumenical movement and to seek unity together.
2. Y. Congar, *Challenge to the Church: The Case of Archbishop Lefebvre*, London and Dublin, 1976, p. 18.
3. *Response to the Final Report of ARCIC I*, London, 1985, p. 4.
4. D. Lapsley, 'Where Is The Ecumenical Movement Going Today?', *Studies*, LXXII, Winter, 1983, p. 301.
5. V. Messori and J. Ratzinger, *Rapporto sulla Fede*, Milan, 1985, p. 171.
6. Fyodor Dostoyevsky, *Crime and Punishment*, Harmondsworth, Penguin, 1951.
7. For the importance of these factors, see W. A. Visser't Hooft, *Memoirs*, London, SCM, 1973.
8. A rather too brief acquaintance with Irish poetry suggests to me that this sense of the ability to move or change is largely absent. As far as I can see only the early sagas and the writings of Patrick Kavanagh and Seamus Heaney offer any vision of the ability to break with the past and shape the future. The cyclic constriction appears as the main theme in Brian Friel's recent play *Translations*, London, Faber, 1981.
9. J. Feiner in H. Vorgrimler (ed.) *Commentary on the Documents of Vatican II*, New York, Herder & Herder, 1968, Vol. II, p. 72.
10. For the background and implications of this decree see A. Heron, 'The Ecclesiological Problem of Inter-Church Marriage' in M. Hurley (ed.) *Beyond Tolerance: The Challenge of Mixed Marriage*, London, Chapman, 1975.
11. This event was recently commemorated at a special service and lecture in St Patrick's Cathedral, Dublin. For an attempt to overcome such 'memories', see the statement on the Revocation of the Edict of

Nantes issued by the World Alliance of Reformed Churches in *Reformed World* 38(6)85, pp. 347-350.

12. Cf. the method and content of T. C. Hammond, *The One Hundred*, London, Society for the Irish Church Missions, 1939, and a Church of Ireland catechism in use into the mid-twentieth century, *Where We Differ from the Church of Rome*.

13. E.g. the Presbyterian Church in Ireland General Assembly of 1966 passed a resolution urging its members 'humbly and frankly to acknowledge and to ask forgiveness for any attitudes and actions towards our Roman Catholic fellow-countrymen which have been unworthy of our calling as followers of Jesus Christ'.

14. *The Exiles*, Manchester, Carcanet, and Dublin, Raven Press, 1984, p. 27; also in his *Selected Poems*, Manchester and Dublin, Carcanet Press, 1985, p. 110.

15. Impressively demonstrated in the collection, H. Meyer and L. Vischer (edd.) *Growth in Agreement*, Geneva, W. C. C., and New York, Paulist Press, 1984.

16. For a discussion of these methodologies, see K. Pathil, *Models in Ecumenical Dialogue*, Bangalore, Dharmaran Publications, 1981, and A. Falconer, 'To Walk Together', *The Furrow*, 34(1)83, pp. 35-42.

17. Sacred Congregation for the Doctrine of the Faith, *Observations on the Final Report of the Anglican-Roman Catholic International Commission*, London, C.T.S., 1982.

18. See C. Daly and S. Worrall (edd.) *Ballymascanlon*, Belfast, Christian Journals Ltd, and Dublin, Veritas, 1978.

19. Impressively outlined in E. Gallagher and S. Worrall, *Christians in Ulster 1968-80*, Oxford, O.U.P., 1982, and E. Gallagher and M. Ledwith, *Ecumenism in Ireland: Experiments and Achievements*, Belfast, Irish Council of Churches, and Dublin, Irish Catholic Bishops's Conference, 1981.

20. Discussions with the Dublin Council of Churches, 1978-81.

21. In A. Flannery (ed.), *Vatican Council II: More Post-Conciliar Documents*, Dublin, Dominican Publications, 1982.

22. See *Register of Local Ecumenical Projects, Ecumenical Officers, Teams and Groups*, London, British Council of Churches, and the various publications of the Consultative Committee for Local Ecumenical Projects in England (CCLEPE).

23. See unpublished M. A. dissertation of Iain Knox, *The Sharing of Church Resources in Ireland*, Hull University, 1975.

24. A survey for the unpublished Essay of the Diploma in Ecumenics of Hull University was undertaken by Mrs Clare O'Mahony to explore how much was being done in the major seminaries in Ireland to implement basic points made in the Decree on Ecumenism and subsequent documents of the Vatican Secretariat for Christian Unity. The findings showed remarkably little action and interest in this with the exception of one seminary in the south east. — 'Education in Ecumenism of the Roman Catholic Clergy in Ireland', Hull University, 1983.

25. Evident in questions of abortion, divorce, and the Forum Report, where no joint approach was conceived.

SISTERS AND BROTHERS

1. Austin Flannery, O.P., (ed.), Dublin, Dominican Publications, 1981.
2. Cf Eagleson and Scharper, *Puebla and Beyond*, New York, Orbis, 1980.
3. J. Dargan, S.J., 'Problems Facing Irish Religious Today', *Religious Life Review*, vol. 23 (1984), p. 233.
4. Jerome Murphy-O'Connor, O.P., 'Religious Life according to the New Code', *Religious Life Review*, vol. 22 (1983) pp. 297-312
5. Cf M.P. Fogarty, L. Ryan, J. J. Lee, *Irish Values and Attitudes*, Dublin, Dominican Publications, 1984.
6. Manmet, Sofield, *Inside Christian Community*, Le Jacq, 1984, p. 41.
7. 'What Women Religious Superiors Discussed with the Pope', *Religious Life Review*, vol. 23 (1984), p. 213.
8. C. Bamford, 'The Heritage of Celtic Christianity' in *The Celtic Consciousness*, Dublin, Dolmen Press, 1981, p. 174.
9. All figures for personnel, vocations, etc., are from the publications of the Council for Research and Development, Maynooth, which is directed by Dr Ann Breslin, S.S.L. Used with permission. These statistical analyses which are annual and also occasional, covering, e.g., ten year periods, are among the most useful and enlightening tools we have for renewal at present. It is not possible to praise them enough, and the comments on the declining numbers and the causes of these are accurate and incisive.
10. Address to Annual General Meeting of the C.M.R.S., 1985, typescript.
11. Jerome Kiely, F.P.M., 'Post-primary Education in Ireland: Challenges and Opportunities', *Religious Life Review*, January-February 1984, pp. 34-51. The whole of this penetrating and important analysis should be read.
12. I am indebted to Fr Paul Byrne, O.M.I., and Sister Regina Gleeson, P.B.V.M., secretaries of the C.M.R.S., for invaluable help in the preparation of this chapter. It incorporates much information and many suggestions of theirs.

THE BOOK AND THE PEOPLE

1. Cf. *The Furrow*, 17 (1966) 163-174.
2. Cf. Michael Maher (ed.), *Irish Spirituality*, Dublin, 1981, pp. 33 - 46.
3. Report No. 18, Council for Research and Development, Maynooth, presented by Austin Flannery, O.P., in *Religious Life Review*, Nov.-Dec., 1984; Jan.-Feb., 1985.

EPILOGUE: WHAT PEOPLE OF GOD?

1. M.P. Fogarty, L. Ryan, J.J. Lee, *Irish Values and Attitudes*, Dublin
Dominican Publications, 1984.
2. Available in Austin Flannery, O.P., (ed.) *Evangelisation Today*,
Dublin, Dominican Publications, 1977.
3. An Address to Past Students of the Institute of Religious Education,
Mount Oliver, 1981.